60 Ways to Make the Most of Your Day

Time Management In An Instant

- Master the art of time planning
- Go for your goals—every day
- Fight distraction and find your focus

Karen Leland & Keith Bailey

CAREER
PRESS
Franklin Lakes, NJ

Copyright © 2008 by Karen Leland and Keith Bailey

TIME MANAGEMENT IN AN INSTANT
EDITED BY JODI BRANDON
TYPESET BY MICHAEL FITZGIBBON
Cover design by Howard Grossman/12e Designs
Printed in the U.S.A.

To order this title, please call toll-free 1-800-CAREER-1 (NJ and Canada: 201-848-0310) to order using VISA or MasterCard, or for further information on books from Career Press.

The Career Press, Inc., 220 West Parkway, Unit 12
Pompton Plains, NJ 07444
www.careerpress.com

Library of Congress Cataloging-in-Publication Data
Leland, Karen.
  Time management in an instant : 60 ways to make the most of your day / by Karen Leland and Keith Bailey.
    p. cm.
  Includes index.
  ISBN 978-1-60163-014-8
    1. Time management. 2. Quality of work life. I. Bailey, Keith, 1945-
II. Title.

HD69.T54.L45 2008
650.1'1--dc22
                                                                  2008021415

For Deborah, until the end of time.
—Keith Bailey

To Jon, for making the time I spend sweeter.
—Karen Leland

Acknowledgments

Many thanks to our agent, Matthew Carnicelli, and the folks at Career Press for guiding us through the process of getting this book to publication. To Liza Ingrasci, the Hoffman Institute, Iris Gold, and Steve Katz for giving us a place to write in peace and quiet when we really needed it. Lastly, to our spouses, Jon Leland and Deborah Coffey, whose patience, support, and encouragement have meant everything.

Contents

Introduction

In the late 1980s, the phrase *work/life balance* began to appear around office water coolers and cubicles everywhere. Today, it's a staple of business books, consulting gurus, and television talk shows. Work-life balance describes the relationship between career achievement (getting ahead, being productive, professional accomplishment, and so on) and personal fulfillment (family, friends, hobbies, contribution, and so forth). But despite all the hype, the last two decades have seen an increase in the average workweek from 43.6 hours to 47.1 hours.

For many people the problem is a catch-22: If you spend more time on your personal life, your work falls behind. But if you spend too much time at the office, your family life and sense of well-being can suffer. Although we don't believe there is a single solution, we do believe that learning to manage time and energy makes a substantial difference in achieving a work-life balance.

The principles and practices in this book come from the time-management workshops we have led within corporations over the

Time Management In An Instant

past 25 years, thousands of employee attitude surveys we have conducted, a review of the most recent research by some of the leading behavioral scientists in the field, and the opportunity to observe our clients up close as they learn to make the most of their day.

Assess Your Time-Management Skills

Are you a time-tamer or a time-waster? To get an idea of your current level of time literacy, answer the following questions using the following guide:

1 = Almost never

2 = Once in a while

3 = Frequently

4 = All the time

1. I create a daily to-do list and then prioritize it._____

2. Whenever possible, I do my most important tasks early in the day._____

3. The state of my desktop inspires me to get work done._____

4. I have specific, written goals for my business and personal life._____

5. I arrive at meetings on time and prepared._____

6. I delegate whatever I can._____

7. My in-basket is under control, and I process the work in it regularly._____

8. I close my office door or take other measures to prevent interruptions when I need to focus._____

9. I know when and how to say no to other people's requests._____

10. I meet my project deadlines._____

11. I can find any information I need within five minutes. _____

12. I spend less than 30 percent of my day putting out fires._____
13. I keep my e-mail in-box organized and up-to-date._____
14. My office files are neat, organized, and up-to-date._____
15. I tackle difficult or unpleasant tasks without delay._____

Total Score:_____

50–60: Congratulations! You are a time-management superstar. You obviously understand the core principles of time management and have been able to translate them into everyday actions. To move to the next level, choose an area that you would like to enhance, and use the information in this book or take a class to help you further develop that skill.

35–49: You have a good grasp on your time, but are losing energy and focus because of a few bad time habits. Review the questions, and focus your attention on the areas where you scored a 2 or lower. Consider reaching out to someone you work with (and trust) to help you identify when you are caught in non-productive time behaviors. Find the specific ways in this book that address the areas you need to improve.

15–34: Your time literacy could use some education. You may be experiencing procrastination, overwhelm, or burnout due to poor time management. Pick one item from the list and, using the principles, practices, and exercises in this book, work on it until your score in that area has increased by a point.

Understand Your Relationship With Time

Philosophers and scientists have been trying to understand time since, well, time began. Just defining it is tricky enough. Some definitions are as simple as "a series of passing moments"; others are more complex, as in the one found on spacetodayonline, which reads: "A human perception defined as the length of an interval separating two points on a non-spatial continuum in which events occur in apparently irreversible succession from the past through the present to the future."

The problem with time doesn't end at our attempt to define it. All the things you tell yourself and believe about time further encumber your relationship with it. For example: Have you ever said or thought, *"There just isn't enough time in the day"*?

Exercise

In the space here, write down the definitions, thoughts, and ideas that you have about time:

_____

_____

_____

Does what you wrote reflect a "use it or lose it" attitude? Does it conjure up a sense of cosmic mystery, or a down-to-earth movement of hands around a clock? Does what you wrote describe a positive or negative relationship with time? Regardless, all of this is what you are trying to manage when you talk about time management. Ask yourself, "*Is this possible?*" or "*Am I crazy?*" Trying to manage time is trying to manage something that nobody fully understands, can define, or even agree on.

If you step back and take a rational look at time, a minute is always a minute, an hour is always an hour, and a day is always a day. Admittedly, if you're organized and focused, time does seem to zip enjoyably and productively by. If you're disorganized and distracted, it tends to creep by slowly, painfully, and often unproductively. But in reality, the actual amount of time remains unchanged.

For example, imagine you have a proposal to prepare for a key client within the next hour. The client's files are easily accessible on your desktop, you have turned off your incoming e-mail alarm, and you've let your coworkers know that you can't be disturbed—all these actions help you to focus and, even though it's an intense hour of work, you get the report done with a sigh of satisfaction.

Now take this same scenario and imagine that you can't easily find the client's files because they are buried under huge piles of unfiled paperwork on your desk, you keep getting interrupted by e-mails, and, at least three times, your coworkers pop their heads in to ask you a question. At the end of the hour, the proposal is only half-finished and you are irritated, frustrated, and now need to stay late.

Same hour, different results. So, although it appears that you can't really manage time, you can mange your experience with it, your energy, your efficiency, and your effectiveness. Have you ever noticed how some people you work with always seem to make the most of their time while others fritter it away?

The time is not the common denominator; the way they manage themselves is. Which person would you rather be?

Get Out of Time Denial

Every April 15th millions of Americans tear their hair out trying to meet the midnight deadline for turning in their tax returns. The reasons for this last-minute rush? Procrastination and denial—specifically, denial about how long it will really take to locate and sort receipts, pull together paperwork, and crunch the numbers so that the forms can finally be filled out and sent on their merry way.

How long does it take you to prepare and fill out your tax return? According to government estimates, it takes taxpayers 28 hours and 30 minutes to complete an average tax return with itemized deductions and income reported from interest, dividends, and capital gains.

This tendency to underestimate the amount of time something takes is not only limited to such serious matters as taxes but can be seen in something as mundane as showing up on time for appointments.

The underlying culprit in all these scenarios is time denial, an inaccurate accounting of the amount of time it will *really* take to get from point A to point B.

To get out of time denial and make a more accurate assessment of the time needed to get somewhere or do something, use the following guidelines:

Work Backward

Begin with the end in mind so that you can figure out, in reverse, what it will take to meet your deadline. Work backward to calculate steps that need to be taken and the time they will take; this helps clarify exactly what needs to get done by when.

For example, say your annual business dinner with the big boss is scheduled for 7:30 p.m. at the hot new restaurant, Café du Posh. Operating in time denial, you plan on leaving the office at 7:00. This would allow a cutting-it-close 15 minutes for driving time and a 15-minute window for getting ready. However, working in reverse, a more realistic time plan would be:

Goal: Dinner reservation	7:30
Arriving 5 minutes early	7:25 (5 minutes)
Parking	7:15 (10 minutes)
Driving, assuming heavy traffic	6:55 (20 minutes)
Getting from your office to your car	6:50 (5 minutes)
Completing work, loose ends, etc.	6:40 (10 minutes)

Without time denial, a realistic departure time becomes 6:40 instead of 7:00. That's a whole 20 minutes that was not accounted for in the first assessment!

Consider the Worst-Case Scenario

A mind in time denial can soften and blur the realities of what it will take to get from A to B. Always plan a 10-percent time factor for emergencies, changes, and delays of game. For example, traffic may be heavier than you imagined, you may have to do an unexpected last-minute task, or parking might prove difficult.

Don't Underestimate the Little Things

A lot of lateness occurs because insufficient attention was paid to the little things, especially those that connect one activity to the next. For example, as you are getting ready to leave, gathering together your wallet, purse, keys, and directions adds time that needs to be accounted for.

Keep an Activity Log

"There are not enough hours in the day." "I don't have enough time to get it all done." "I have more on my plate than I can handle." These are just a few of the popular phrases in the litany of time complaints business people proffer on a daily basis. Despite the very real fact that, in some cases, you do have too much to do, with too little time, a recent survey by America Online and *Salary.com* revealed that the average employee admits to wasting more than two hours every work day. Which activities are eating away at American workers' precious productivity? According to the survey, the top time-wasters include:

Surfing the Web	44.7 percent
Chatting with co-workers	23.4 percent
Doing personal business	6.8 percent
Spacing out	3.9 percent
Running errands	3.1 percent
Personal phone calls	2.3 percent
Applying for other jobs	1.3 percent
Planning personal events	1.0 percent

"But I hardly do any of the above," you loudly protest. *"I never waste time at work!"* The truth is that most people (even you over-achieving overachievers) have some bad time habits that eat into your efficiency and effectiveness.

One way of discovering how you really spend your time—including where your bad habits may lie—is to keep a detailed daily activity log for an entire week. Here's how it works.

Step 1: Write down all your activities.

Each day, from the moment you get to work to the moment you leave, write down everything you do (business or personal) and how much time you spend on each item. Pretend you are an impartial auditor sent to create a detailed and accurate an overview of how you use your time. For example, if your first 15 minutes in the office are taken up with chatting about last night's Yankees game over a cup of coffee in the break room, log it. If you then spend the next 20 minutes checking e-mail, log it. And so on. By the end of your day your log might look this way:

Start	Finish	Activity	Time Invested	Return	Cost
8:30	8:45	Chatted with Fred, got coffee	00:15		
8:45	9:05	Checked e-mail	00:20		
9:05	9:35	Web "research" on vacation packages to Aruba	00:30		
9:35	9:45	Prepared for Operations meeting	00:10		
9:45	9:55	Checked e-mail	00:10		
9:55	11:30	Weekly Operations meeting	1:35		
11:30	12:00	Informal debrief with Jim from Operations	00:30		
12:00	12:45	Lunch	00:45		
12:45	1:05	Chatted about meeting fallout	00:20		
1:05	1:15	Phone call with Aruba vacation specialist	00:10		
1:15	2:10	Listened and responded to voice mails	1:05		
2:10	2:35	Looked for last quarter's budget numbers!!	00:15		
2:35	2:45	Waited for Budget meeting to begin	00:10		
2:45	4:15	Budget meeting	1:30		
4:15	4:30	Evaluated today's activity log	00:15		
		"C" TOTAL:			

Step 2: Assign each item a return value.

At the end of each day, review your log and assign a return value of A, B, or C to each line item. Use the following as a guide.

A = I received a high return on this item toward an important objective.

B = I received a medium return on this item toward an important objective.

C = I received a low return on this item toward an important objective.

Step 3: Determine the cost of "C" items.

In order to figure out the cost of each item, start by determining your hourly wage. If you are a consultant, accountant, or attorney, and already get paid by the hour, this is no problem. If, however, you are paid a yearly salary, use the following formula to make an educated guess about what your hourly rate would be. Assuming a 40-hour work week:

$$\frac{\text{yearly salary}}{2080} = \text{Hourly wage}$$
(number of hours in a year)

Once you have determined your hourly wage, figure the cost for each "C" item you have listed by multiplying the actual amount of time invested in that item by your hourly wage. For example, assuming an hourly wage of $40, a 15-minute "C" item would have a total cost of $10. Enter this amount in the cost column.

Note: The focus is on "C" items because these items usually offer little or no return, and are relatively unproductive.

Step 4: Analyze your daily activity log.

To see how much time during a particular day was spent on low-priority items, add the time invested for your "C" items together and place at the bottom of the log. Now do the same for your "C" item costs.

Time Management In An Instant

Based on an wage of $40 per hour, your completed activity log would look this way:

Start	Finish	Activity	Time Invested	Return	Cost
8:30	8:45	Chatted with Fred, got coffee	00:15	C	$10
8:45	9:05	Checked e-mail	00:20	B	
9:05	9:35	Web "research" on vacation packages to Aruba	00:30	C	$20
9:35	9:45	Prepared for Operations meeting	00:10	B	
9:45	9:55	Checked e-mail	00:10	B	
9:55	11:30	Weekly Operations meeting	1:35	A	
11:30	12:00	Informal debrief with Jim from Operations	00:30	B	
12:00	12:45	Lunch	00:45	B	
12:45	1:05	Chatted about meeting fallout	00:20	C	$13
1:05	1:15	Phone call with Aruba vacation specialist	00:10	C	$7
1:15	2:10	Listened and responded to voice mails	1:05	B	
2:10	2:35	Looked for last quarters budget numbers!!	00:15	C	$10
2:35	2:45	Waited for Budget meeting to begin	00:10	C	$7
2:45	4:15	Budget meeting	1:30	B	
4:15	4:30	Evaluated today's activity log	00:15	B	
		"C" TOTAL:	1:55		$66

This activity log shows that almost two hours, and $66, were spent on 'C' items during this day. In other words, two hours of your time went into activities that produced very little return for your efforts.

Step 5: Review your week.

To find out more about your time-effectiveness, complete an activity log for each day of the workweek. You may be surprised by the amount of time you spend gossiping with co-workers, opening mail, dealing with interruptions, and other "C"-value work. Use a review of this log to become aware of where your time is actually being spent, any bad habits you have fallen into (say, surfing the Net for airline deals 30 minutes a day) and any adjustments you may want to make in how you currently invest your time.

Exercise

Make five copies of this blank activity log, and for one week keep track of how you spend your time.

Start	Finish	Activity	Time Invested	Return	Cost
		"C" TOTAL:			

Apply the 80/20 Rule

Vilfredo Pareto, an Italian economist in the early 20th century, is credited with the discovery of the 80/20 principle. Way back in 1897 (before cell phones, e-mail or the Web) Pareto observed that 80 percent of the wealth was owned by 20 percent of the population. Not much has changed since then, and Pareto's theory of disproportion has been widely applied to almost every aspect of business, from quality control to time management. Here are some of the ways that the 80/20 Rule might be impacting you and what you can do about it:

The Rule: 80 percent of your goals are achieved by working on 20 percent of your tasks. Identify which of your to-do's will move you the farthest towards accomplishing your goals and make those a top priority.

The Rule: 20 percent of your efforts produce 80 percent of the results. Learn to recognize which of your labors make the most effective use of your time.

The Rule: 80 percent of the value you receive from business reading comes from 20 percent of the material. Determine which business magazines, journals, books, and other materials consistently produce the most value, and drop the rest.

The Rule: 20 percent of your co-workers give you 80 percent of the support you need. Identify who has your back at work, and return the favor in kind. Make a priority of maintaining your relationships with these people and acknowledging them for the ways in which they make your work life easier.

The Rule: 80 percent of the value your customer receives relates to 20 percent of what your company does. Make the effort to determine which are the most important measures your customer judges you on, and invest your time to make those top notch.

The Rule: 20 percent of your time-management habits cause 80 percent of your productivity problems. If you really look, most of your time issues can be boiled down to one or two bad habits (such as lack of prioritization or multitasking). Identify your worst ones and work on improving those.

Exercise

For one week, make note of where the 80/20 Rule is showing up in your worklife. At the end of the week, determine how you could adjust the way you organize, delegate, or execute actions to make the most of Pareto's principle.

6

Achieve Your Goals Every Day

Wouldn't it be wonderful if, after setting your goals, all you had to do was kick back and wait for the universe to deliver them to you? Although you will occasionally be graced with this effortless miracle of instant achievement, more often than not, your goals require self-effort to make them happen. Too often, the pull of urgent matters at work forces you to focus on items that need your immediate attention, and your less-pressing (but important) goals sit ignored. The key to making your goals a reality is to take four steps to consistently and regularly invest time towards their achievement.

Time Management In An Instant

Step 1: Start by identifying one goal that you would like to achieve, but have not found the time to work on. For example:

Goal: Close two new clients by the end of the month.

Step 2: Next, take a look at your calendar and physically block out a specific time period when you plan to work on this particular goal. In general, you want to schedule a period of no less than 15 minutes and no more than an hour.

Hot Hint: Turn your cell phone to silent and turn off the ding on your e-mail.

Step 3: Now that you have a time period blocked out, create a to-do list of actions you can get done within that time frame toward achieving the goal. For example:

- Go through the business card pile on my desk and e-mail potential clients.
- Call Bob at the Coffee Cup Corporate Headquarters and ask if he has anyone he could refer me to.
- Send out a pricing sheet and brochure to the potential client who left a voice mail on my phone yesterday.
- Compose a draft press release about our latest product for Internet distribution.

Hot Hint: Stay focused on the goal you have chosen to work on and avoid getting seduced into working on some other to-do during your planned time.

Step 4: Do this every day, week, or month for the rest of your life. Regularly reviewing and setting aside time to work on your most important goals will transport you out of hope that they happen and into probability that they will.

Hot Hint: In the early stages of achieving a goal, particularly a large, lifetime one, you may find reading, attending classes, or other educational activities useful.

In this stage you are not so much working on the goal as you are getting ready to dive in.

Design Goals in All Areas of Life

According to a 2006 telephone study conducted by Opinion Research Corporation, more than 80 percent of U.S. adults (18 years and older) make New Year's resolutions in the following categories: health, finance, work/life balance, and time management.

Having goals in all areas of life (not just work-related) leads to a greater work/life balance, a sense of time being richly spent, and a greater sense of accomplishment. Under the day-to-day pressures of family life and business obligations, it can be easy to develop tunnel vision when setting goals. Use the following exercise to stimulate your thinking and brainstorm goals in a multitude of life locales.

Exercise

Be sure to let your imagination wander and write down whatever comes to mind. In this first part, it's important not to edit yourself; you may be surprised at some of the things you come up with. After you're done with the whole exercise, you can go back through and cross out the goals that are just pipe dreams!

Time Management In An Instant

Career
Promotion, new skill, sales targets, entrepreneurial ideas, etc.
One Month: _____
Six Months: _____
One Year: _____

Health
Exercise, weight management, diet, medical conditions, etc.
One Month: _____
Six Months: _____
One Year: _____

Relationships
Family, friends, dating, spouses, children, co-workers, etc.
One Month: _____
Six Months: _____
One Year: _____

Creativity
Writing, painting, photography, art, music, hobbies, cooking, etc.
One Month: _____
Six Months: _____
One Year: _____

Finances
Budgeting, investments, savings, taxes, charity, etc.
One Month: _____
Six Months: _____
One Year: _____

Home
Garden, decorating, buying, selling, remodeling, etc.
One Month: _____
Six Months: _____
One Year: _____

Recreation
Hiking, golfing, running, sports, vacations, etc.
One Month: _____
Six Months: _____
One Year: _____

Personal Development
Self-awareness, spirituality, further education, etc.
One Month: _____
Six Months: _____
One Year: _____

> ### State Them in the Positive
>
> There are two ways to approach articulating a goal: as something you are moving *toward,* or something you are moving *away from.* Stating a goal in the positive (I want to weigh 125 pounds) is a way of building a bridge to your future; stating a goal in the negative (I want to lose 20 pounds) is more akin to burning the bridge behind you. Think of one goal you have been talking about in the negative and turn it around to a positive statement of accomplishment. How does this change the way you feel about the goal?

Beware the Stop-Goal

Whenever you set your sights on a goal (regardless of its size or scope), you also create the possibility for its polar opposite: the stop-goal. A stop-goal is anything that looks as if it might get in the way of you achieving your objective, and usually involves feelings of fear, confusion, overwhelm, worry, discomfort, and doubt. The stop-goal is always in relative proportion to the size of the aim you have set, so a small goal usually sparks a relatively small amount of stop-goal, and a large goal often dredges up a large amount of stop-goal.

For example, let's say you've set a relatively small goal to clean out your file drawer. You open up your long-forgotten folders and confront the ugly truth about all the papers you have been unceremoniously stuffing in there for years: forms you were supposed to fill out but never did, important phone numbers scribbled on burrito wrappers, reports you meant to review but didn't.

As you move deeper into the drawer, overwhelm descends and you start to panic. Your brain clamors for air and silently screams, "Abandon ship! This was not a good idea!" Sitting there, surrounded by a mountainous mess of paperwork and your own dark thoughts, you are smack dab in the middle of a stop-goal. A strong desire takes hold to shove everything back in, slam the drawer, and walk away.

Whenever you are faced with the inevitable stop-goal, you have an option about where you put your attention. If you focus on the stop-goal (and, in this case, walk away), your time will have been wasted. If, however, you recognize the stop-goal but make a conscious choice to focus on your objective, the outcome will be a clean file drawer. As your goals get bigger and bolder, the stop-goal also grows.

For example, let's say you set a significant goal of forming a task team to develop and implement a plan to improve quality company-wide. After inviting a highly considered group of players to join the team, you receive a few rabid responses of "I don't think we need this sort of thing corporate-wide. Let each department handle it themselves." Several other people leave a voice message saying they are "just too busy to participate." The e-mail from the person you had hoped to head up the committee briskly informs you that she has taken another job and will be gone by month's end. Despite your best intentions, here you are face-to-face with a sizable stop-goal.

The optimistic enthusiasm you started with has now mutated into skepticism. "Fine," you think. "If no one else cares, why should I?" Your may even begin to wonder if you should even be working at this company.

Once again, you have a choice about where you focus. If you zero in on the stop-goal you might decide that this was just too much to take on and quit the project. On the other hand, if you keep your eyes on the prize you can use the power of your commitment and your negotiation skills to find ways to work around the roadblocks presented.

Too many people do not realize that the stop-goal is a natural part of any worthwhile achievement, and consequently give up too often and too soon.

Learn to see the stop-goal as a sign you're on the right track and ask yourself, "What actions can I take to work through these obstacles?" and "Who do I know who could offer me helpful advice or assistance?"

Lay Out Your Long-Term Goals

It's not surprising that, in this multitasking, interruption-driven, and nanosecond world, goals get limited to what can be achieved within a short period of time. A day, a week, a month—rarely do individuals think one, five, or 10 or more years out.

Directing your attention to such far-off future horizons may seem disconnected from the workload on our shoulders right now, but it's one thing to look back at your day having accomplished a few worthwhile things and quite another to look back over a lifetime of dreams fulfilled and major aims achieved.

Pursuing long-term goals (five years out or more) gives you greater overall direction and helps inform the choices you make daily. Not having them is like being in a rudderless boat: You will end up somewhere—but it may not be where you would like. Taking some quiet time to slow down and think about what you really want in your life can bring a clarity, direction, and satisfaction that will impact the years ahead.

Begin by taking a step back and reflecting on your personal values. These are the principles and standards of behavior you truly consider important in your life.

Time Management In An Instant

Some examples include:

    Achievement.

    Balance.

    Creativity.

    Flexibility.

    Freedom.

    Fun.

    Generosity.

    Honesty.

    Leadership.

    Learning.

    Optimism.

    Philanthropy.

    Teamwork.

Next, take a look at these values. Do you currently have any long-term goals associated with them? For example, if one of your values was *learning,* a congruent goal might be to *become fluent in French.*

Finally, ask yourself if you are actively and consistently working on the accomplishment of these goals. If the goal is to *become fluent in French,* for example, some of the tasks that appear on your to-do list might be:

      Plan a trip to Paris for a three-week language school.

      Take a beginning French class at your local community center.

      Purchase an online French language course.

      Join the French group at your local Rotary.

10

Make Your Goals Specific

In the famous children's book *Alice in Wonderland,* Alice asks the Cheshire Cat, *"Would you tell me, please, which way I ought to go from here?"*

"That depends a good deal on where you want to get to," says the Cat.

Goals, as both the Cat and any savvy business professional know, provide a clear guideline for choosing how you are going to invest the time and energy you have available in any given minute, hour, day, or lifetime.

Yet despite what seems to be common sense and top-notch advice from some of the world's best thinkers, most businesspeople still don't take the art of goal-setting seriously enough. Thinking about or telling a colleague what you'd like to have happen in the future is a worthy start, but it won't necessarily pay off at the finish line.

Ask almost any group of 100 people to raise their hands if they have a *goal* to have more money, and 90 percent of the room will enthusiastically wave their paws high up in the air. But point out that finding a quarter on the ground could easily fulfill this goal, and that same 90 percent will shake their heads and say *"But that's not what I meant."*

In order to increase your chances of meeting your goals, try to make them as specific as possible (including setting a time frame). Being precise in the goals you pick helps you know how much progress you have made and exactly when you have arrived. Consider this example:

A general goal might be stated as *I want to improve my presentation skills.*

But how will you know whey you have arrived? What specific measures tell you that you are, in fact, a better speaker?

A better-defined goal might be: *Within the next six months, I want to improve my presentation skills by feeling more comfortable using eye contact, weaving in stories, and integrating PowerPoint into my speeches. These efforts will result in my evaluations going from a 3.0 to a 3.5.*

If the thought of creating goals that are this detailed and precise brings up the dread of being locked into a direction or time line that you can't change, relax. You create your goals, and you can change them—at any time. Just because you generate a goal does not mean that it's carved in stone. If circumstances change and the aim is no longer appropriate, you are free to adjust or even abandon it.

Write Them Down

Motivational guru Brain Tracy put it best when he said, "Goals in writing are dreams with deadlines." Unfortunately, a recent survey by Day-Timer reveals that 32 percent of American workers never plan their daily work! Goals that remain in the recesses of your mind may be good ideas, but they often fail to make an appearance in the light of day. For those people who do put pen to paper, they often find that this simple step gives them the push they need to act.

Set Solid and Stretch Goals

Most serious goals come in two flavors: solid and stretch. **Solid goals** are those objectives that offer you some challenge, but in essence are practical and doable (for example, taking a family vacation to Disneyworld, saving enough money for your child to attend a good college, or finishing a 5K race within 30 minutes—when your last, best time was 35). Solid goals make up an important part of your achievement inventory and can give you a tremendous feeling of accomplishment.

Stretch goals, on the other hand, require more of a leap of faith in what you are capable of creating. They come from your deeper dreams, imagination, and desires, and require conviction in your ability to rise to the challenges they present (for example, doubling your small business revenues within a year, going back to school for your law degree at 50, or finishing a 5K race within 20 minutes—when your last, best time was 40). Stretch goals force you to grow and expand in ways that you would not have without the motivation and momentum the goal provided.

Solid Goals Are...	Stretch Goals Are...
Clearly achievable through work and planning.	Less certain to be achieved even with work and planning.
Practical and reasonable.	Somewhat impractical and often unreasonable.
More or less within your current comfort zone.	Outside your current comfort zone.
A logical next step to take.	A calling that requires a leap of faith.
Accomplished by following a step-by-step predictable path.	Accomplished by forging new paths that are usually unpredictable.
Often created out of a sense of need or desire.	Often created out of a sense of calling or vision.
Require reasonable self effort.	Breakthroughs in self-effort and self-perception.
Challenges with a high chance of success.	Challenges with a greater risk of failure.

For many people, the idea of stretch goals (and all that they require) seems a bit too scary to take on. Remember that time keeps on ticking by; your choice is how you are going to fill it. If you aim for the moon and only reach the stars, you still got farther than you would have had you not set your sights so high in the first place.

Exercise

Thinking about your life, what are some of your current *solid* goals?

_____

What are some of your current *stretch* goals? If you don't have any, brainstorm here what a few of them might be. A few good questions to consider are:

What dreams do you have that you have not taken action on?

_____

Do you have a long held desire to be, do, or have something that won't go away?

_____

If money and time were not obstacles, what would you want?

_____

If you knew you could not fail, what would you attempt to do?

_____

Is there something you have been longing to learn since you were a kid?

_____

Support Your Goals

A 2006 Day-Timers, Inc. study of more than 1,000 adults showed that people achieve their goals when there is a powerful combination of internal motivation and external support. The top motivations and support cited by respondents who were successful at reaching their objectives included the following:

- 86 percent noted determination to make it, even when it got hard.
- 76 percent made a commitment for the long haul.
- 76 percent accepted setbacks and got back on track.
- 71 percent found that visualization was an aid to success.
- 59 percent rewarded themselves for success.
- 57 percent told other people.
- 44 percent set up reminders.
- 40 percent created a step-by-step plan.
- 39 percent asked for help and didn't do it alone.

Joseph Grenny, author of *Influencer: The Power to Change Anything,* agrees and says that his research has shown that people who used at least four of the following six strategies are four times more likely to change their behavior and achieve their goals.

1. **Deliberately practice.** It's not enough to just have a goal to write a novel, be named salesperson of the year, or climb Mount Everest. Reaching any goal, regardless of size, involves action and practice, as much as intention and clarity. By identifying what specific behaviors and habits you would need to develop and/or change,

and making a point to practice each one on a regular basis, you will develop the new skills you need to achieve your objectives.

2. **Create cues.** Many of the goals you want to achieve require new attitudes and practices. Posting prompts about the behaviors you want to change in highly visible places will remind you to keep these new habits front and center in your mind.

3. **Give yourself incentives.** Too many people wait until they have reached the finish line before rewarding themselves. Instead, celebrate the small wins all along the way and reward yourself for achieving milestone accomplishments towards the overall goal being realized.

4. **Find encouragement.** As Ralph Waldo Emerson said, "Our chief want in life is somebody who shall make us do what we can." When it comes to achieving your goals, success is usually not a solo effort. Having a buddy who or support group that can celebrate your successes, help you maintain perspective when things are not going exactly as planned, and prop you up during the rough times is an invaluable part of reaching any goal.

5. **Get coaching.** Distinct from joining a group or finding a buddy, coaching is a more formal approach to getting support. Many people find it useful to pay a professional coach (someone who has experience or knowledge about the area they are working on) to help them negotiate their way through the learning curve of achieving their objective. Others find a mentor, someone who wants to contribute their time, experience, and knowledge, as a way of giving back.

   Either way, the coach you choose should be someone you trust to give you feedback on what you are doing right and specific suggestions for how you might improve.

6. **Embody your values.** Make sure the goals you choose are anchored in something that is of core importance

to you. Goals that are other people's good ideas, or that you feel you think you *should* have, are the most likely to fail. By setting your sights on goals that are a reflection of your most important values in life, you will have an authentic desire to achieve them.

Broaden Your Definition of Finished

Here is the hard, cold reality: Nobody—not even the most efficiently awesome time gurus on the planet—get everything that they planned done in one day—except sometimes. It's the nature of work that, despite all preparation and the best intentions, some items scheduled for today must be put off until tomorrow. For example:

You have an "A" priority item on your to-do list to call back a customer regarding his recent bill. You have tried to reach him several times, with no luck. He returned your call, but you were out at a business lunch. Back and forth telephone tag ensues, and you are about to leave for a meeting that will last the rest of the day. After one more valiant but unsuccessful try at reaching him, you give up and move the item to tomorrow's to-do list.

At this point you have two choices: You can feel bad about the item being unfinished, get dragged down by a nagging sense of incompletion, call yourself names, and delve into the depths of shame at having to transfer the task to tomorrow, or you can broaden your definition of what finished means.

If you look up the word *finished* in the dictionary, some of its synonyms include: over, ended, done, and complete. This traditional definition of finished implies that you have moved successfully from point A to point B. Mission accomplished. Done. Finito.

Such a narrow and limited description can be expanded to include synonyms for the word *complete,* such as whole, inclusive, broad, and wide-ranging. These allow you to create a sense of closure on all your day's to-do items—even the ones you don't get finished.

Sound like a contradiction in terms? Au contraire. Though you may not be able to *finish* every item on your to-do list, you can *complete* every item, by knowing where you stand. Where you stand with each item is based on making a clear decision about the next action you are going to take. Are you going to do it now? Okay. It's done and complete. Are you going to assign it to someone else? Great. Pass it along, and it's complete. Are you going to abandon it? Fair enough. Cross it off your list, and be done with it. Are you going to transfer it? Excellent. Move it to another day, week, or month, and rest easy in knowing that you have it planned for the future.

Items that are delegated or transferred usually require follow-up at some point and won't be finished until they are done or abandoned. However, for that day, they can be complete because you know your next step in their achievement. The only option that won't give you a sense of completion is ignoring the task and not making a firm decision about its next step.

Generate Energy With Your To-Do List

Whenever you complete something (big or small) an eruption of energy bursts forth and livens up your day with a sense of accomplishment. For example, think of the thrill you get when you put a check mark next to an item on your to-do list, finally finish up that six-month project, or even clean out your pencil cup.

Although time can't really be managed (an hour is an hour), your energy can. One of the underlying principles of time management is that closure creates energy. Any time you finish something (regardless of its size) you will increase the amount of liveliness you experience. This can manifest itself in many ways, including feeling relieved, uplifted, inspired, renewed, energized, delighted, thrilled, and proud.

Continually creating closure can help you stay motivated. One of the best sources for producing ongoing energy is your average, everyday to-do list.

Assume that you have a daily to-do list that resembles this:

Task	Priority
Do expense report for Thailand trip	B
E-mail boss regarding next week's sales conference	A
Call district manager to discuss problem on Adams account	A
Clean out last month's complaint files	B
Schedule meeting with team for product launch	C
Send card to Carol to thank her for her help last week	B
Go to bank and get foreign currency for upcoming trip	C

Standard operating procedure for many people is to work their way (in between interruptions) through the list, and at the end of the day realize their gains and give a mental nod to their efforts. The tasks that fell to the wayside are often transferred to the next day's to-do list.

The problem with this system is that it overlooks the ongoing opportunity to generate energy all day long by recognizing what got done—*on the spot.* The key is to acknowledge the completion of the item (regardless of size or priority) as soon as it's finished by:

- Putting a check mark next to the item.
- Crossing it off the list.
- Highlighting the item.

Hot Hint: If you use an electronic to-do list you may also move the item to a different list of completed to-do's or delete it.

Assume that you have already been at work for a few hours and several of the items on your to-do list have been completed. Here's your updated list:

Task	Priority	✓
Do expense report for Thailand trip	B	
E-mail boss re next week's sales conference	A	✓
Call district manager to discuss problem on Adams account	A	✓
Clean out last month's complaint files	B	
Schedule meeting with team for product launch	C	
Send card to Carol to thank her for her help last week	B	✓
Go to bank and get foreign currency for upcoming trip	C	

By taking a few seconds to essentially say "this item is done," you charge up your closure battery, throughout the day, instead of just at the end. Try it and see. Open up today's to-do list. Are their any items on it that you have finished but not recognized by checking off? If so, do it now! How did that make you feel?

Add Your Interruptions

If you find yourself fielding a lot of interruptions (with requests from co-workers, customers, or your boss) resulting in new to-do items during the day, add them to your list and check them off when completed. By recognizing these newly arrived entries as complete, you can turn them from time-stealers into energy-creators.

Minimize Unfinished Business

Everyone has at one time or another experienced both the energetic lift of getting things done and the down-and-out doldrums of unfinished business. Anything that lacks closure (no matter how small) has the potential to drain your liveliness and steal your focus. This can manifest itself as feeling worried, stressed, depressed, overwhelmed, grumpy, guilty, frustrated, and tired. Here's a typical example of how you can start off in the morning with lots of energy and good intentions, but how the little things around you, left incomplete, can sap your spirit and drain your energy:

To begin with, you wake up refreshed and raring to go. There are a lot of exciting things happening at work these days, and your job puts you right in the middle of the action.

Driving to work, you stare out at the traffic, tossing over in your mind the proposal that you promised to send yesterday but didn't.

Arriving at work, you walk into your office and notice the broken printer (which you have been meaning to take to the recycling center for the past few months) still shoved in the corner.

As you open up your e-mail, your eye catches the blinking yellow light on the postage machine, which has been flashing its "low postage" warning for the past few days.

Turning your attention to your desk, a stack of folders needing to be sorted and filed commands your attention. Holding them down is a makeshift paperweight: your half-filled mug of cold coffee—just where you left it last night before you left.

Time Management In An Instant

You turn on your computer and attempt to locate the proposal you should have done yesterday, which you must get done today. Unfortunately your desktop is covered with files and it's difficult to locate the proposal.

Frustrated at not being able to find the proposal, you check your e-mail. Several messages from yesterday need to be answered, and overnight a few, new urgent ones came in. You need to attend to them but you are suddenly feeling so tired that you swoop up your mug and head straight for the coffee machine.

What happened to all that vim and vigor you started with just a few hours ago? Drained away by the droves of unfinished business.

Why is it that such seemingly little things can have such a big impact? Think of your brain as a computer with a limited (a very large, but limited) amount of memory. The fuller it becomes, the less capacity it has to efficiently process new information. Regardless of whether your incomplete items are at home or work, they all contribute to how much focus you can bring to bear on the tasks at hand.

Exercise

You can clear away the mental clutter and create more space by making a list of those items that lack closure and making a plan to get them done—or deciding that you are never going to get them done and declare them complete. Use the following list to help you identify a few general areas where unfinished business often lurks. Circle each item as either:

- In good shape (IGS).
- Could use work (CUW).
- Needs serious attention (NSA).

My closets and drawers are organized and uncluttered.   IGS CUW NSA

If not, what needs to be done?

My home repairs are up-to-date.	IGS CUW NSA
If not, what needs to be done?	

My finances are in order.	IGS CUW NSA
If not, what needs to be done?	

My office space is neat and organized.	IGS CUW NSA
If not, what needs to be done?	

My computer files are organized and easy to find.	IGS CUW NSA
If not, what needs to be done?	

I am up-to-date with my phone calls and e-mails.	IGS CUW NSA
If not, what needs to be done?	

I am up-to-date on my commitments with clients.	IGS CUW NSA
If not, what needs to be done?	

I am up-to-date on my commitments with co-workers.	IGS CUW NSA
If not, what needs to be done?	

I have no conversations that I am putting off.	IGS CUW NSA
If not, what needs to be done?	

Take a few minutes and look over your "could use work" and "needs serious attention" items. Choose two items that you find yourself thinking about a lot, and commit to taking some action on them within the next week. Actually sit down and schedule some time (in your planner, or on your PDA or computer) to get them done. Continue this process every week until all your CUW and NSA items have moved into the IGS column.

Choose the Perfect Planner

One of the cardinal rules of top-drawer time management is keeping your mind clear of clutter by writing down all your tasks and to-do's. Some people put stylus to screen and keep track via their smartphone, PDA, or computer. Others choose the old-fashioned method and put pen to paper—which may include a legal pad, Post-It notes, and occasionally the back of a bus ticket.

If you are part of the group dedicated to paper, the chances of misplacing or losing your information will be greatly reduced if you purchase a time planner. Time planners are a great way to keep critical information about projects, goals, and tasks right at your fingertips. With dozens on the market, some of your core choices are:

1-Week-Per-Page

Pros: Having seven days condensed onto one page makes for a thin, lightweight and portable book that will easily fit into your purse or briefcase. This is the perfect planner if you have a small amount of to-do's and only the occasional appointment.

Cons: Having one week squeezed into a page doesn't provide room for you to jot down notes, capture ideas, or enter more than a small handful of to-do's.

1-Day-Per-Page

Pros: These planners often split the page, offering you both an appointment calendar and a to-do list—a useful layout if you need more space for taking notes.

Cons: Devoting a page to each day adds to page count and hence bulk to your book.

Hot Hint: If your need for a calendar is minimal, look for a page design that devotes more space to the to-do list.

2-Pages-Per-Day

Pros: This page layout, when open, provides one page for your calendar and one page for listing tasks—allowing you ample room for scheduling your day, listing a slew of tasks, and recording notes, phone numbers, and other important details.

Cons: This is the bulkiest planner design, and its portability may become a problem if you like to travel light.

Size Really Does Matter

Full-Size (8 1/2" x 11")

This is the big Kahuna of time planners and is designed primarily for those people who write a lot, who rarely leave their office, and for whom portability is not an issue.

Medium-Size (5 1/2" x 8 1/2")

The most popular, all-round size, the pages are big enough for the busiest of people, but allow for portability, without a pack-horse.

Small-Size (4" x 6")

Highly portable, but the tradeoff is small pages that may cramp your style and consequently your thinking.

Mini-Size (3" x 5")

Too small and impractical for most businesspeople, this size is useful only if you have few appointments, a couple of tasks each day, and no need for taking notes.

More information about the four most popular planners can be found at their Websites:

- Time/Design (*www.timedesign.com*).
- DayRunner (*www.DayRunner.com*).
- Franklin Covey (*www.FranklinCovey.com*).
- DayTimers (*www.daytimer.com*).

Consider Both Paper and PDA

A personal digital assistant (PDA) may sound like a neat and tidy human being that sits outside your office, but is in fact a small gizmo that lives in your purse or pocket and often does double duty as a phone, camera, Web browser, e-mail receiver, calendar, to-do list, database, and address book (can-opener, flashlight, and smoke detector currently in development). Face-to-face with this digital Swiss army knife of time management, you might think that there was no other option but to go high tech, but many people, after using a PDA for a period of time, are going back to the analog world—that is, paper. If you're sitting on the fence and can't quite decide which solution would work best, take the following comparison test by placing a check mark next to the features that most apply to you. As with all things high-tech, the side with the most features wins.

I like using a stylus or small keyboard.		I like putting pen to paper.	
My job keeps me pretty mobile.		I mostly sit at my desk.	
Looking at a small screen is not a problem for me.		I like to be able to read and write my action items clearly.	
I rarely need to take notes in my job.		My job requires that I take a lot of notes.	
I do not attend many meetings.		I attend a lot of meetings.	
My action items change during the day.		My action items are static and rarely change.	
The small work space does not inhibit or hinder me.		I like the space that a page gives me.	

I need something small and portable.		The weight and size of a time planner book don't bother me.	
I love to use high-tech gizmos.		I am not in love with high-tech gizmos.	
Using up battery capacity would not be a problem.		Using up battery capacity could be a problem.	
Having a backup on my desktop computer is very important to me.		Having no backup, or a less convenient and slower one, doesn't worry me.	
I need the alarms to remember appointments.		I do not need alarms.	
Being able to store several years of information is necessary for my work.		I do not need to store information from other years.	
I continually add, change, or erase addresses.		Now and again I add an address to my list.	

Sync and Swim

For many people, the major advantage of a PDA (or smartphone) over a time planner is the ability to synchronize it with their computer. Syncing keeps all information up-to-date on both gadgets, and provides you with a backup should your cuddly little high-tech companion jump from the 10th-floor window because of burnout.

The most popular program for the Windows platform is Microsoft Outlook. Outlook provides robust task management, calendaring, e-mail, memos, and contacts, all of which can be synced either directly (such as with a Blackberry) or indirectly (using third-party software such as Intellisync).

For Mac users, iCal and Address Book, which are part of the system software, have proven to be the most popular. Syncing with an iPhone requires no third-party software and is relatively easy. However, one big drawback (at the time of this writing) is that the iPhone does not provide a task-management tool (save the rudimentary notes), so those who want to track their tasks and prioritize them via your phone are out of luck.

Put Together a Workable Planner

Is your time planner as thick as the New York yellow pages and as heavy as a brick? A profusion of pages and paper scraps stuffed inside can make your planner unwieldy and untidy, and make you less efficient and more disorganized. Part of the problem is that planners come with a plethora of pages, some of which—though nifty at first glance—don't really do much for you in the way of productivity, but do take up valuable real estate in your book. What you do need are the following basics that allow you to sanely manage your day, week, and month:

To-Do List

These are the daily pages where you list your appointments and tasks for the day. If you're not the type who writes your to-do's down more than a week ahead, then carry only seven daily pages at a time. At the end of one week, take out the old pages (you might want to archive them) and add the next seven days of fresh pages—being sure to transfer any items that were not finished from last week.

Monthly Calendar

Although you may not plan your to-do's several months in advance, chances are that you will need to book appointments weeks and months ahead of time. If you carry at least six months' worth of a monthly calendar in your planner, you can easily schedule next week's important meeting and next quarter's even-more-important vacation.

Notes

Always have blank paper on hand in your planner so that you can capture any notes that don't fit into your appointment calendar or to-do list. This way, when you are in the big meeting and get bored, you will at least have a place to doodle and make your grocery list. In the event that the meeting proves super-productive and a whole new slew of notes or to-do's gets created, you would use a projects page.

Projects

For easy access, it's a good idea to give each project you are working on its own separate page(s). As you plan for a certain task associated with the project to be completed on a specific day, move that task to your daily to-do list.

Hot Hint: Your projects should include personal as well as business projects, and are a good place to keep your list of short- and long-term goals.

Expenses

The perfect place to keep track of the checks you write, cash you spend, and expenses you incur. For security reasons, it's best not to enter bank account or credit card numbers on these pages.

Hot Hint: Small hole-punched receipt envelopes are available in a variety of sizes.

Contacts

Often the last section of your book, this is the place to keep frequently used names and phone numbers. It's a good idea to keep a hard or electronic copy of these, just in case (heaven forbid) your planner is misplaced.

Hot Hint: Because most database software gives you the option of printing your information in various sizes for different planners, you can store your information on the computer and print it out for your planner.

> **Avoid Planner Creep**
>
> To stop planner creep, don't use the pockets of your book as a permanent filing system, but for temporary storage only. For example, if you gather business cards at a networking event, transfer the information to your database, contact pages, or card file ASAP.

19

Capture Your Open Items

Open items are those tasks, to-do's, projects, goals, ideas, and actions (business or personal) that you need or want to do, but have not yet done. They may tug at you to get done today, or be as far off in the future as retirement. The trick is to gather them together by *writing them down* so that you don't have to waste valuable mental real estate trying to keep track of them.

Think of your brain as a computer hard drive; it can only hold so much memory. When a hard drive reaches its capacity, it starts to slow down and wonky things happen. By capturing your open items on a list, your brain is freed up to focus on what's in front of you right now. The ideas and to-do items that comprise these lists come from a variety of different sources, including:

- Conversations with family, friends, and business associates.

- Something you read (book, magazine, business brief, research paper, and so forth).

- Items you receive in the mail (a brochure, invitation, pamphlet, and so on).

- E-mails.
- Classes you take.
- Conferences you attend.
- Voice mail.
- Professional groups you belong to.
- Meetings you attend.
- Your in-basket.
- Your desktop.
- Your file drawers.
- Your closets, cupboards, and cabinets.

If you only do one activity from this book, make it this one. Just taking the time to capture all the open items in your life and write them down can dramatically improve your ability to focus and get things done. You can do this all in one sitting (in which case you will need at least a day) or in short spurts. To drain your brain, do the following:

- **Go through all your physical spaces at work and home.** Look through your desk drawers, desktop, in-basket, closets, cupboards, shelves, and file drawers, and make a master to-do list of anything that needs to be done based on what you see. For example, as you look in your file drawer, do you need to clean out last year's financial file and store the receipts; make file folder labels for the most recently added documents; or follow up with a potential client whose business card you found stuck in one of the folders?

- **Go through your electronic spaces.** Sort through your e-mail in-box, PDA, and voice-mail messages, and add any action items to the existing master to-do list that you are not going to handle immediately and that are not recorded elsewhere. Examples include an e-mail from a colleague requesting you make a few changes to a report you wrote, a voice message from your brother about possible dates for a family reunion, and an e-mail from the professional association of crawfish-catchers announcing their annual crab feed fund-raiser.

- **Go through your own brain.** Look through your own mind and, using the source list provided here, write down any relevant to-do items. Once you have done this final emptying out, you can keep this system squeaky clean by adding to your master to-do list anything that pops into your head.

Hot Hint: Some people prefer to keep a master list of all these various and sundry to-do's, and transfer them to a daily or weekly to-do list as needed. Others prefer a detailed breakdown of the master list into more defined categories.

Jott Yourself

Have you ever been out and about and wanted to write yourself a note, but did not have a piece of paper or pen handy? Who hasn't! Enter Jott, a service that converts your voice into e-mails, text messages, reminders, lists, and appointments—all through the simple use of a telephone. Check it out at *http://jott.com/*.

Create To-Do Lists

Although a daily to-do list helps you administer short-term action items, there are three additional categories of to-do lists that help you capture and manage business and personal longer-term tasks, goals, dreams, commitments and projects. They are:

Monthly To-Do List

The monthly to-do list is the perfect place to write down objectives that are not urgent, but that are important and contain multiple steps.

For example, let's say it's February and you want to "update finances." Though not a specific action item itself, there are lots of related one-step tasks this generates that you could put in your weekly or daily schedule, including:

- Make an appointment with the attorney to revise your will.
- Call your stockbroker and review all your current positions.
- Complete the retirement planner questionnaire your accountant sent you.
- Apply for house refinance at current lower rates.
- Balance your checkbook.

Project List

The project list is a perfect holding place for items that take a longer period of time (months and years instead of days and weeks) to come to fruition. For each project you would have an overall project title and associated list of major milestones. For example, if your project was to remodel your office, the major milestones might include:

- Develop overall budget.
- Select architect to oversee the job.
- Survey staff to determine most desired and needed changes.
- Come up with initial renderings.

Each of these milestones would then have a list of specific tasks connected with them, which you would place on your monthly, weekly, and daily to-do lists.

Someday To-Do List

Everyone has one: the "someday when I retire, make more money, have more time, get around to it" wish list. These are the good ideas you want to get done someday. Even if they seem as if they're an eternity away, write them down. You may or may not ever get around to them, but, by having them captured, you won't spend your cerebral energy trying to hold them in your mind.

Plan Your Daily To-Do's

If you're similar to most people, the first thing that pops into your mind when you think of time management is a daily to-do list. Hardly a novel idea, time-management gurus and business big shots alike have been touting their use for an eternity. There is just something so satisfying about writing an item down and then checking it off.

But beyond the feel-good factor, daily to-do lists help you allocate your time, prioritize your efforts, and focus your energies. One recent survey by Kelton Research reported that 73 percent of people who use a to-do list reduce their stress simply because they have everything written down. The daily to-do list is a straightforward system for writing down what you want to get done on a given day. To be effective:

- List items that have to get done, as well as items you want to do.
- Create a roadmap of what you think you can realistically achieve in a day, not a fantasy of what you wish you could.

Hot Hint: An over-ambitious to-do list will leave you feeling disheartened and de-motivated at the end of the day.

- Plan items that can be completed in one or two action steps that day.
- Build in flexibility so you are able to adjust as emergencies and interruptions arise.

- Save time by grouping similar activities (such as phone calls, errands, and e-mails) together so they can be done all at once.

- Choose several items of different priorities, including a few that are not urgent, but important to get done.

- At the end of each day transfer items that did not get done to the next day's to-do list or to another date in the future.

- Be mobile. A to-do list that sits on your calendar at work won't help you when you are out and about. For this reason many people like a combination of paper and online to keep track of their to-dos.

- Periodically review the list during the day to keep the items front and center in your mind.

Despite its ease of use and obvious benefit, many people still don't avail themselves of this essential time-management tool. Another survey by Day-Timers, Inc. found that only 59 percent of Americans *begin* their workday by reviewing a daily action plan. If you are one of the 41 percent who don't, be smart and start writing.

22

Retool Your Priority System

In his book, *CEO Logic: How to Think and Act Like a Chief Executive,* Ray Johnson writes, *"Prioritizing is the answer to time management problems—not computers, efficiency experts, or matrix scheduling. You do not need to do work faster or to eliminate gaps in productivity to make better use of your time. You need to spend more time on the right thing...."*

Though many people prioritize their tasks, most use a system that is based on emergency and crisis. They assign items an A, B, or C (or 1, 2, or 3) based on which fire needs to be put out first! The problem with this method is that it only addresses the actions that impact you now, and not the ones (such as your goals and projects) that affect you in the future. To retool your priority system, start by distinguishing between tasks that are urgent and those that are important:

- **Urgent** tasks are those that require immediate action and attention.
- **Important** tasks are those that move you closer to an important goal.

Urgent, But Not Goal-Related

Everyone has urgent tasks that must get done, but oftentimes these tasks may not be important. In other words, they may produce the lowest return (for the time and energy you invest) toward your most important business and personal goals. A priority system that makes these *urgent but not goal-related* items an "A" keeps you stuck in solving emergencies or maintaining status quo, but prevents you from paying sufficient attention to the items that move you toward your goals and objectives. To retool your priority system, assign items that are urgent but unimportant (that is, not goal-related) a "C" priority.

Hot Hint: Items that fall into the category of not goal-related and not urgent (such as routine errands and paperwork) would also be a "C" priority.

Urgent and Goal-Related

Some items on your to-do list are both urgent *and* related to your goals. In other words, the return you get (for the time and energy you invest) in these items is high. To retool your priority system, assign items that are urgent and important (that is, goal-related) an "A" priority.

Goal-Related but Not Urgent

Think of one thing that—if you did it on a regular basis—would improve the quality of your life. Chances are that this item, whatever it is, is important, but not urgent. Too often the actions that have a very high return for the time and energy invested sit by the wayside, because they are not nagging at you to get done. To retool your priority system, assign items that are goal-related but not urgent a "B" priority.

Hot Hint: To make the most of your time have at least one "B" item on your to-do list every day.

Let's say that some of your most important business and personal goals include:

- Cross-train service staff in sales skills.
- Increase sales by 20 percent this quarter.
- Learn to water ski.
- Plan a family trip to Hawaii next summer.

Using the criteria in this section to prioritize, your to-do list might look this way:

Task	ABC
Make bank deposit (urgent, but not goal-related)	C
Research Hawaii hotels (goal-related, but not urgent)	B
Process new sales orders	A
Develop initial cross-training schedule	B
Return call to unhappy customer (urgent and important)	A
Research water ski schools on the Web	B

Exercise

Write down in the following chart about seven to-do items you got done yesterday. Using the priority system in this section, assign each one an A, B, or C priority.

Task	ABC

23

Utilize the Four D's

The daily to-do list. It's both the bane of freewheeling, spontaneous entrepreneurs and the savior of compulsive, high-power players everywhere. Whichever side you psychologically fall on, the list remains one of the best time-management tools around. Writing down all your intended achievements for the day is only part of the story, however. Deciding on what to do with each one is the other. To maximize your effectiveness, efficiency, and energy, for every item on your list decide on one of the Four D's.

Do

Some items on your daily to do-list excite and inspire you to seize the day and make them happen—now. Others just have to get done by a certain deadline. In either case, for tasks that must find their way to the finish line today as the Nike commercials say, "Just Do It."

Key questions: Is this an item that can be easily and quickly done now? Is this an item I have set aside this specific period of time to do? Is this an item that would take less than five minutes to complete?

Key caution: Oftentimes things land on your desk that you had not planned to handle and were not expecting. The temptation to get them done and over with can be strong. However, if doing this item now means putting off a higher-priority, more important, or more critical item, consider the short-term rush of instant gratification against the long-term reward of achievement.

Dump

Some actions make their way through your calendar, transferred from day to day or week to week. Here's a hint: If you find yourself continually putting off an item, it's usually because the task is:

- Too big and needs to be broken down into bite-sized chunks.
- Not clearly defined enough for you to take action on.
- Something you don't really want, need, or intend to do.

If this last reason fits, there is no shame in saying "no" to an action—especially one you thought up. If, however, the item came from your boss, though it may be tempting to dump it, it's not a good idea.

Key questions: Do I really need or want to do this? Is this something I am committed to or just a good idea? Do I have this item on my list out of desire or guilt?

Key caution: In the face of too much to do, with too little time and too little resources, it's easy to panic and abandon ship on tasks that in the end would have been worthwhile to pursue. Before abandoning ship on any item of significance or impact, reflect on your priorities and how important its getting done is towards your overall goals and objectives.

Delegate

Just because you thought the task up does not mean you have to be the one to execute it. One of the best strategies for instantly creating time is to transfer an item to another's in-box. Considerations, of course, need to be given to the other person's availability, ability, and willingness, but always consider the option of passing on a piece of the work to someone else.

Key questions: Do I really need to be the one to do this item? Is there someone else equally or more competent I could pay to do this or pass the task onto?

Key caution: When it comes to delegation, out of sight should not mean out of mind. Just because you pass the baton on to someone else, you are still ultimately responsible for getting it done. Be sure to schedule a follow-up on any such items in your calendar.

Defer

Many items onto your daily to-do list are there just as a holding place for an idea or task that could be accomplished within a greater time frame. By reflecting on your priorities, goals, and commitments, you can more easily determine which bits and pieces don't require action today, but can be put off until tomorrow. The key here is to immediately write down the item on another date you plan to get it done.

Key questions: Is it essential or important that this be done today, or can it wait? Would there be any serious negative consequences if I delayed doing this item?

Key caution: Many items that are important to the achievement of your long-term goals are not pressing or urgent. Beware of the tendency to always be deferring these in favor of more in-your-face, immediate items. Instead, try scheduling a specific date and time to work on these goal-forwarding, but non-critical items.

The Four D's in Action

One-way to actively invoke the Four D's everyday is to mark them on your to-do list. By taking a decisive action on each task, you complete it for that day.

In this example, every to-do item on the list has been categorized as:

✓	Done
→	Deferred
D	Delegated
X	Dumped

Task	Priority	✓
Do expense report for Thailand trip	B	→
E-mail boss regarding next week's sales conference	A	✓
Call district manager to discuss problem on Adams account	A	✓
Clean out last month's complaint files	B	→
Schedule meeting with team for product launch	C	D
Send card to Carol to thank her for her help last week	B	✓
Go to bank and get foreign currency for upcoming trip	C	X

Exercise

Take a look at your to-do list from yesterday and today. Which items got done? Check them off now. Are there any items you have decided you should abandon? Cross them off or put an X next to them now. What items can you delegate (and to whom)? Put a D next to them now. Which items need to be deferred to another day, week, month, or even year? Move them and then put an arrow next to them now. How do you feel? Relieved, energized, more complete? Making a firm decision about your next action on an item is one of the keys to energy management.

24

Learn From the Masters

Throughout history great philosophers, business masterminds and even presidents have pondered this question: *How can I best use my time?*

Their respective answers underlie many of the prioritization systems in use today.

The Psychologist

In 1943 Abraham Maslow wrote his famous paper, "A Theory of Human Motivation." Maslow's idea was that people are most able to cope with the larger issues of their lives (achievement, creativity, problem-solving, and so on) when their fundamental needs (food, warmth, shelter, safety, and so forth) are taken care of. This hierarchical view of human needs inspired the **POSEC** method.

Prioritize your time according to the goals that you want to accomplish in life. If you start by knowing where you are going, it's easier to get there.

Organize yourself by creating structures that allow you to meet your basic need to feel stable and secure in both your finances and family. This could mean setting up a regular Friday-night dinner with your family or having a certain percentage of your paycheck automatically removed to a savings account.

Streamline the things that you have to do but don't necessarily like to do (such as chores) by simplifying them or making them more efficient. For example, do all your routine errands (bank deposit, post office, grocery store) in one outing, rather than in separate trips.

Economize by reducing the amount of time and energy you invest in things that are not urgent and that you view as low-priority. For example, you may want to clean out your file drawer, but don't need to spend a whole day doing it.

Contribute by giving your time and energy back to the community, a charity, or a good cause. Many people find that, when they have prioritized, organized, streamlined, and economized, they have a natural inclination to contribute to a bigger purpose.

The Business Guru

Stephen Covey, in his best-selling book *First Things First* (Free Press 1994), tells a story that illustrates the importance of making your most important tasks the highest priority. In the book Covey describes a time-management teacher filling a mason jar with large rocks and asking his students if the jar is full. When they respond yes, he proves them wrong by adding gravel to fill in the spaces between the rocks. Asking if the jar is now full, the students are not so sure. He then adds sand and water to fill in the remaining in-between spaces. When the teacher asks what the point of the demonstration is, the students' reply is that, if you look hard enough, you can always fit more into your life. No, retorts the teacher, who explains that the point is that, if you don't put the big rocks in first, they will never fit. Do you tend to make time in your day for the gravel, sand, and water, but never find time for the big rocks?

The President

Dwight D. Eisenhower was quoted as saying, "What is important is seldom urgent and what is urgent is seldom important." This philosophy is the basis for the Eisenhower method of prioritizing, where tasks are sorted by the following criteria:

- Tasks that are unimportant and not urgent should be done later, deleted, or delegated.
- Tasks that are important and urgent should be done now and not delegated.
- Tasks that are unimportant and urgent should be done now and, whenever possible, delegated.
- Tasks that are important and not urgent should be given a high priority, scheduled, and not delegated.

Cultivate Time-Efficient Conversations

Everyday conversations—a salesperson talking over the phone with a potential client, a customer service representative solving a customer's problem face-to-face, a purchasing manager working out the details of a contract with a vendor via e-mail—are to a business what an engine is to an automobile. Without them, nothing moves. Yet, despite their obvious importance, many conversations at work seem to go nowhere (fast) and don't produce the desired results (slow). Knowing what kinds of conversations create action and which create inertia is a crucial skill for making the most of your day.

Conversations that contain a request usually fall into the action category. Depending on the other person's working style, he or she may express a request more or less strongly and specifically. For example:

More specific: Kim, I need you to get in by 7:30 tomorrow morning so that we can finish the inventory by noon. Can you do that?

Less specific: Rana, I don't think I can get that inventory done by tomorrow. Would you be able to help me out?

The more specific, clear, and strong a request is, the more time-efficient it becomes, because it leaves nothing to chance, and therefore the possibility of it getting done on time and to spec is that much greater. To insure that your requests are as time-friendly as possible, add the following:

Specific Outcomes

A request that is stated in too general terms carries with it the potential to waste time, energy, and money. For example: *I am speaking at a conference next week, and I need all the information you can get me from Research and Development.*

Not knowing what is really wanted, the person receiving the request might work overtime to create a 100-page report that is indexed and bound, and take time away from another higher-priority project. Or, he could jot a few, quick notes in an e-mail and send it off. In either case, the speaker might not get what he or she really wanted and needed. Most of your co-workers are not certified mind readers, and, though they may be able to guess right about some of what you want, some of the time, it pays to be clear up front. For example: *I am speaking at a conference tomorrow and I need a two-page overview on our latest product from Research and Development.*

Time Frame

A specific time frame, agreed on by you and the other person, helps guarantee that you will get what you want when you want it. For example: *I need last month's sales report as soon as possible.*

This request could be interpreted many different ways because "as soon as possible" might mean next week to one person, or as soon as I'm done with everything else on my plate to another. A more time-efficient time frame would be: *I need last month's sales report by noon tomorrow.*

Background Information

When making a request, don't assume that the other person knows as much about the background details as you do. Look at this example:

Jill sends an e-mail to her coworker Mike in accounting saying, "*I need my expense invoice reimbursed by the end of the week.*"

Mike, having no background information from Jill, has to look up the details, which results in a one-week delay of the check getting paid.

Here is the same request with the background information added:

"*My expense invoice, number 3421 for $651.23, was submitted on 3/15/08. Due to an internal accounting error it was not paid on time. Would it be possible to get it paid by the end of this week?*"

Conversations which contain these kinds of specific requests are a far cry from conversations that go around and around. These types of inertia conversations are one of the biggest time-wasters in the workplace, because they are often centered on personal opinions with no commitment to resolution. They most often rear their ugly head in four specific forms at work. Be wary: They will lead you down the path of lost productivity.

- **Wishing conversations.** These pie-in-the-sky discussions focus on desires but don't move anything forward. For example: *Every quarter we have to do the* *inventory, and every quarter I am hard-pressed to get it done on time—I wish they'd make the process easier!*

- **Judging conversations.** These accomplish venting—and nothing more. Everyone has a tendency to make negative judgments, and these conversations never transform into anything productive. For example: *The last company I worked for had a very good inventory process. They really knew what they were doing—not like this place.*

- **Whining conversations.** Different than complaining (which, if done responsibly, can lead to action), whining is rarely directed at anyone who can do anything about the situation. For example: *I hate this inventory process. It never seems to get any easier. I can't stand the software we have to use; the whole process needs to be upgraded. I dread this time of year.*

- **Talking about taking conversations.** If you have ever sat in a meeting where there was a lot of discussion but nothing seemed to happen, and you left wondering what all the hot air was about, then you understand this fruitless and frustrating form of inertia conversation. Unlike brainstorming, which is a discussion that eventually leads to action, discussion for discussion's sake maintains the status quo and is ultimately frustrating.

Identify Your Interruptions

You're hard at work on that top-priority proposal when your co-worker from the next cubicle bursts in and asks if you've got a moment to help him fix the copier. Reluctantly, you stop what you are doing to rescue your colleague. Twenty minutes later you're back at work on your proposal, but your former focus has fizzled.

How often would you guess that you get interrupted at work by external sources (including other people, phone calls, e-mails, and so on)? How about the internal, self-interruptions caused by multitasking? In both cases, probably more often than you realize.

A recent study by Gloria Mark, a professor at the University of California, Irvine, found that workers spend on average only 10.5 minutes on a task before being interrupted, and that it takes an average of 23 minutes and 15 seconds for them to return to the original task. The study also showed that 56 percent of that time the distraction is caused by an external force, and 44 percent of the time by self-interruption.

Exercise

To find out how often you *really* get interrupted at work (and by what), schedule a 45-minute window to specifically focus on a project or task that you can do in your office and ideally at your desk. Using a clock, stopwatch, or timer, as soon as you begin, keep track of every interruption (external or self-generated) that occurs and log it. For example, let's say your 45-minute work window began at 1:00 p.m.

INTERRUPTION LOG—EXAMPLE

Interruption	Self/Other	Time Began	Time Ended	Total Time
Call home	Self	1:05	1:06	1 minute
Phone rings	Other	1:10	1:20	10 minutes
Get coffee	Self	1:30	1:35	5 minutes
Co-worker question	Other	1:40	1:44	4 minutes
E-mail ding	Other	1:43	1:45	2 minutes
Total				22 minutes

Analyzing the above, of the 45 minutes of focused time scheduled, 22 minutes (or 48 percent) were taken up with interruptions. Use the blank Interruption Log here to keep tabs on yourself for a few sessions. When you have a couple of days of data, analyze your interruption patterns and ask yourself:

1. How often do I *really* get interrupted when I try and focus?
2. Are my interruptions more internal or external?
3. What kinds of things most frequently interrupt me?
4. What am I doing (or not doing) that contributes to my being interrupted?
5. How are these interruptions affecting my focus and productivity?

INTERRUPTION LOG

Interruption	Self/Other	Time Began	Time Ended	Total Time
Total				

Overcome Multitasking Madness

On an average day you probably e-mail off a memo to co-workers, surf the Net for the latest and greatest technology, fill out sales reports, and sit in on several conference calls—usually all at the same time. A recent report from the Institute of Psychiatry at the University of London found that, when workers are constantly juggling e-mails, phone calls, and text messages, their IQ falls 10 points. Another study by Rubinstein, Meyer, and Evans found that, when people switched back and forth between tasks, there was a substantial loss of efficiency and accuracy, in some cases up to as much as 50 percent.

In today's non-stop work environment—courtesy of PDAs, e-mail, instant messaging, and so forth—the five projects people used to manage in a day have tripled to 15. Too much input and too little control have left the modern worker struggling with way more than he or she can productively handle. To overcome multi-tasking madness try the following:

Turn Off Technology

The ding of an e-mail coming in, the buzz of the Blackberry. All these seemingly harmless inputs can tempt you to stray from the job at hand and multitask.

Create Designated Task Times

By setting aside a selected time period to do all your phone calls, e-mails, or errands at once, you will reduce the amount of time you spend going back and forth between them.

Make the Most of Your Morning

In her book *Never Check Email In The Morning* (Fireside 2005), author Julie Morgenstern recommends that people avoid checking e-mail for the first hour each day and instead spend the time working on an important task or project that requires focus.

Put a System in Place That Lets You Capture All Incoming To-Do's in Writing

Instead of feeling pressure to do the item now (lest you forget), your brain can relax, secure in the knowledge that you have the item identified and stored.

Maintain a Desktop In-Box

Don't just rely on your electronic mailbox or filing system. By putting a physical in-box on your desk you will be able to temporarily place items that need your attention in a location where you can easily find them.

Plan Some Open Space

Instead of booking every minute of every workday, leave some open time when you can catch up on anything new that comes in, or process old items that have been hanging around.

Don't Multitask, Multi-purpose

If all this talk about concentration and singular focus makes you break out in a sweat, relax and check out the cousin of multitasking: multi-purposing. By doing two things at once (combining tasks) you can save time and effort. Here are a few examples: listening to business books on CD while driving, catching up on reading memos or reports while on the treadmill or stationary bike, having a working business breakfast, and plowing through paperwork on the plane or at the doctor's office.

28

Fight Distraction and Find Your Focus

Do you have a second? Can you take a few minutes to look at this? Are you able to meet with me now? Common questions, but, if you say yes too often, your focus and productivity can suffer. In today's high-pressure workplace, learning to manage interruptions is a key time-management skill. Here are a few ways disruption-weary workers can fight distraction and find their focus.

Propose a Later Time

The next time someone strolls into your office asking, *"Do you have a few minutes to talk?"* say *"I'd be happy to, but not right now."* Instead of assuming that you have to drop everything you are doing and respond on the spot, make an appointment with that person for later in the day.

Set a Time Limit

If the matter is urgent, find out how much time the person needs, and negotiate to give him or her that much (or less) and no more at the moment. If future discussions are needed another meeting can be scheduled. Doing this helps you keep interruptions to a minimum and educates everyone around you to be more efficient in how they communicate.

Bypass the Story

To limit the impact of an interruption, encourage people to bypass the story and get to the point. Ask if they can summarize in one sentence what they need from you, the solution they propose, and the specific time by which they need it.

Change Locations

One way to prevent interruptions is to make it harder for people to find you. If you have a particular project that requires a lot of concentration, consider commandeering an empty office or conference room that is not in use and working from there.

Schedule Open-Door Hours

Don't have an open-door policy that encourages people to interrupt you whenever they feel like it. Instead schedule, post, and promote open-door hours on certain days. With a little encouragement, most people will wait until these times to talk to you about non-urgent matters.

Store Supplies Elsewhere

Are you the keeper of the ballpoint pens and file folders? If everyone comes into your office to access files, offices supplies, or other materials, move them to a location where you will not be continually disturbed by their retrieval.

Don't Interrupt Your Interruptions

Don't compound the disruption of your first interruption by adding a second one on top of it. For example: You are reading at your desk, riveted as you review the latest changes in employment law, when suddenly the phone rings (interruption #1). It's your co-worker asking you to check and see if his last expense invoice was paid; you oblige. You're just about to end the conversation and get back to your reading when he asks if you can take a minute to send him a hard copy of the new expense policy (interruption #2). You oblige again. Now you are two interruptions away from your original task. Unchecked, this can grow to three, four, or more!

Don't Be Unavailable

The point of limiting interruptions, especially during times when you need to focus, is to improve your productivity and effectiveness. It is not to never, ever talk to anyone in your organization again. Always keep in mind the bigger picture of what benefits your co-workers, department, and company.

Executive Strategies

A 2007 study of 247 senior level executives, conducted by the Center For Creative Leadership, asked interviewees what strategies they use to bring more concentration into their cubicles:

- 29 percent: Close their door including posting *do not disturb* signs.
- 18 percent: Prioritize their calendar by scheduling specific times for work appointments and open time.
- 14 percent: Use their executive assistant to screen calls and people, only letting through the most important.
- 13 percent: Turn off their cell phone, office phone, and Blackberry, and only take urgent calls.
- 12 percent: Telecommute from home or work off site, including planning what specific work they are going to do on an airplane or in an airport.
- 6 percent: Limit e-mail by setting specific times to check it, turning off the ding, and using their assistant to pre-screen e-mails.
- 4 percent: Arrive early, stay late, or work on weekends so they can get work done when no one else is around.

Don't Get Caught in the Yes Trap

You're standing around the water cooler minding your own business when your co-worker from the next cubicle starts pleading with you to organize the Dunk the Clown booth at next month's company picnic. You quickly connect the dots and realize that, between the upcoming sales presentation and your aunt's annual visit, the answer must be no. As you open your mouth to say, "I'm sorry. I wish I could, but I can't," you do a 180-degree turnaround, and out spills, " I would be happy to."

This small, two-letter word doesn't have to be so difficult to say if you learn to say "yes" to the right things and "no" to the wrong ones. This is easier to do if you understand the three yes traps and their solutions.

Trap 1: Good Candy

Remember years ago there was always one house on the block that handed out really good Halloween candy? Your plans always included a visit to that address! Even as an adult, no one wants to feel they are missing out, so you say yes for fear that, if you decline, you might be passing up an opportunity.

Smart Solution: When you want to participate but the timing or scope is wrong, offer an option or ask for a rain check:

"I'd love to be asked at another time."

"Can I have a rain check on that?"

"Maybe next week, month, year...."

Trap 2: Bad Guy

Saying no is not just a problem of the willy-nilly and weak-kneed. Feeling an internal pressure to say yes has nothing to do with education, success, or smarts. The fear is that, if you say no, you might be perceived as unfriendly, uncooperative, or not a team player.

Smart Solution: Let the other person know you empathize with his or her situation or feelings:

"I know how important this is, and I feel bad, but I'm not in a position to say yes."

"I feel bad, but I won't be able to help right now."

Trap 3: You Like Me

Wow! They want you to be in charge of the company softball team. Of course you are flattered; who wouldn't be? Everyone wants to be liked. The opportunity to be part of a group is rewarding, but even things that are fun can become a burden if you're overextended.

Smart Solution: In this 24/7 can-do culture, the pressure to say yes to everything can be overwhelming. Create a boundary that lets other people know when you have reached your time, energy, and attention limits:

"I have too many other things on my plate right now."

"I have competing priorities."

"I really don't have the time."

Exercise

Are you stuck in the yes trap?

How often are you caught in the yes trap? You might be surprised. The more of these questions you answer with "true," the more you need to recover your ability to just say no!

Circle true or false:

1. I often say yes for fear of missing out on something.

   True/False

2. I frequently worry that if I say no, I might hurt someone's feelings.

   True/False

3. I often think if I say no, I may be viewed as uncooperative or not a team player.

   True/False

4. I frequently feel guilty when I say no, especially if I can see what is needed.

   True/False

5. I want people to like me, so I often say yes, even when I don't really have the time or energy.

   True/False

6. In general, it makes me feel uncomfortable to say no.

   True/False

30

Break the Habits That Hold You Back

Bad time habits don't suddenly appear overnight; instead they develop slowly over time, as certain behaviors—repeated over and over—begin to overlay the way you work. The good news is that, with awareness and effort, you can break your bad habits and turn time-wasters on their head.

Step 1: Name your bad habits.

Take a look at the following list of widespread habits and check off any that apply to you. Feel free to add your own at the end.

- _____ Procrastinating to the point of lost productivity and opportunity.
- _____ Having a disorganized office, desk, or workspace.
- _____ Keeping a chaotic filing system.
- _____ Having messy piles of paperwork.
- _____ Operating in crisis management.
- _____ Over-promising and under-delivering.
- _____ Not meeting deadlines you agreed to.
- _____ Not keeping your promises about time.
- _____ Being continually late for meetings and appointments.
- _____ Constantly interrupting yourself by checking e-mail.
- _____ Arriving at meetings unprepared.
- _____ Not keeping a daily to-do list.
- _____ Not prioritizing.
- _____ Failing to delegate.
- _____ Multitasking to the point of distraction.
- _____ _____
- _____ _____

Step 2: Identify the negative impact.

Take a look at the items you checked and choose one that you would be willing to put in the effort to change. What negative impact has this bad habit had on your business (and perhaps personal) life? For example, let's say you checked "*arriving at meetings unprepared.*" The negative impact on yourself and others might include:

- You feel unable to make a decision in the meeting.
- You can't fully contribute to the conversation.
- The progress of the group is hindered.
- You lose credibility with your co-workers.

My bad time habit is:

_____

The negative impact it has is:

_____

Step 3: Brainstorm positive results.

Next, think about the positive results that could come about if you changed this habit. How would turning this habit around impact you? How about your co-workers, family, and friends? For example:

If I arrived prepared for meetings, it would reduce my stress level, and I would feel more knowledgeable about the issues and be able to make faster decisions. Others would see me as a responsible team player.

The positive results that would come out of my changing this habit are:

_____

Step 4: Break down the habit into specific steps.

If you look closely, all negative habits are made up of a series of steps and the thoughts that go along with them. For example, when informed about an upcoming meeting:

You write it in your calendar, and tell yourself that you will prepare for it later.

As the meeting gets closer you start to get stressed and notice that you don't have the time you need to adequately prepare for it.

You tell yourself that you are not prepared because you had other things to do that couldn't wait.

Your negative time habits also consist of a string of actions and thoughts that go along with them. Write them here.

_____

_____

Step 5: Create alternative actions.

Now get creative and think of some alternate ways you could act and think about the actions to turn them into a good time habit. For example:

At the same time as entering the meeting in my calendar, I will also schedule a 30-minute block of preparation time.

I will consider this appointment with myself a high priority and not let other urgent items crowd it out.

I will schedule my computer alarm to notify me 30 minutes before the start of the meeting so that I have time to look over the meeting agenda and my notes before I arrive.

My alternative actions include:

_____

31

Size Up Your Delegation Skills

How do you manage your time when there doesn't seem to be enough hours in the day to get everything done? Because the responsibility that comes with most managers' jobs is almost always greater than their individual capacity, delegation is an essential tool for time management. Assuming that you're sold on the necessity of being a demon delegator, a good place to start is by evaluating your current delegation attitude and skill set.

Exercise

Read through the following statements and circle the number that best reflects your current assessment of yourself. Use the following as a guideline:

1 = Never
2 = Sometimes
3 = Much of the time
4 = Almost always

1. The jobs I delegate usually get done the way I want them to.

    1 2 3 4

2. I take the time to delegate the right task to the right person.

    1 2 3 4

3. When I give clear instructions and they are not followed, I see it as an opportunity to improve *both* how I communicate *and* train my staff.

    1 2 3 4

4. The work I delegate gets done as well as if I had done it myself.

    1 2 3 4

5. I consider my staff's current workload before delegating.

    1 2 3 4

6. When I delegate work, I almost never have to do it over.

    1   2   3   4

7. When I delegate, I explain the parameters of how a job should be done.

    1   2   3   4

8. I delegate both routine and non-routine tasks to my staff.

    1   2   3   4

9. I believe that delegation saves me time.

    1   2   3   4

10. In many cases, my staff can do the work I delegate to them better than I can.

    1   2   3   4

Total Score _____

32–40: Congratulations! You are a skilled delegator, and see assigning tasks and projects to your staff as a way to save you time and develop their abilities. To improve even further, try your hand at delegating something more strategic or higher priority to a trusted member of your staff. If the item you delegate requires you to closely coach and mentor your staff member, all the better. Teaching a subordinate a new skill is satisfying and will free you up to work on other projects.

21–31: You are doing a decent job at delegation and, with a little more effort, could reap big time-saving rewards. Use an activity log to determine what specific tasks you could delegate to your staff on a daily basis and begin to do so. Consider taking a class on delegation or asking another manager in the company who excels at this skill to coach or mentor you.

10–20: Delegation is not your strongest suit and is probably hindering your time-management efforts. Start by reviewing the questions and see if you can find a trend. Are you a poor delegator because you don't take the time to properly pass things on? Do you distrust other people to do the job as well as you would do it? Try to identify the main underlying reason why you don't delegate (or do it poorly), and check out the other delegation ways in this book to help you improve.

32

Decide Who to Delegate To

Once you have gone through the process of picking and choosing which tasks on your massive to-do list can be passed on, the next question is to decide whom they should be delegated to. Remember that, although you may be ready and raring to download, not all staff members are willing or able to receive your requests. Part of your job is to pave the way for delegation by building up the other person's skills (his or her ability) and by motivating him or her (his or her willingness) to take on the task.

To increase willingness:

- Delegate items that are associated with things you know that staff member likes to do.

- Include the staff member in the process of setting the goals and then delegating items associated with these goals.

- Explain the importance of the delegated item to the person, and clarify how his or her participation will make a difference in its accomplishment.
- Explain how doing the delegated item will benefit the staff member directly.

To increase ability:

- Delegate items that will challenge the person's current capability, but are still within his or her existing skill set.
- Provide formal training that will help the person take on the delegated item.
- Offer to coach (or get a coach for) the person to help him or her deliver on the job delegated.
- Have the person work with you on a similar project, so he or she can develop the skills necessary to take on future delegated items.

The Right Job for the Right Person

Does this person have the time to take on this task?

Does he or she have the skills and experience necessary to complete the task well?

Would this person need training in order to do the task? (If yes, do I have the time necessary to bring him or her up to speed?)

Is this a project he or she would find interesting and/or aligned with his or her work interests and goals?

Does this person have the self-management and independence needed to do the job I want to assign to him or her?

Exercise

Choose one item that you want to delegate. Evaluate your existing staff and fill in their names in the appropriate boxes on the next page.

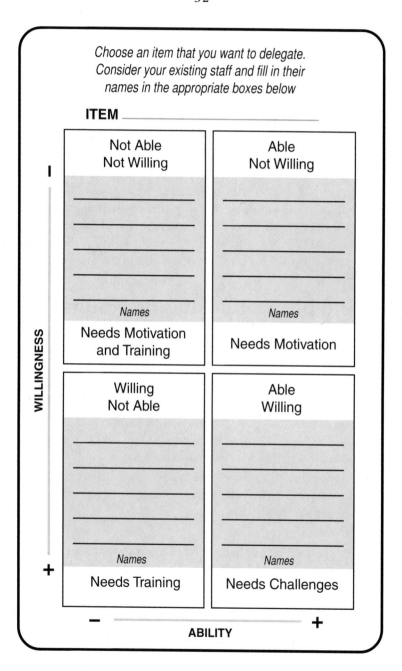

*Choose an item that you want to delegate.
Consider your existing staff and fill in their
names in the appropriate boxes below*

ITEM _____

WILLINGNESS

I

Not Able Not Willing	Able Not Willing
_____	_____
_____	_____
_____	_____
_____	_____
_____	
Names	*Names*
Needs Motivation and Training	Needs Motivation

Willing Not Able	Able Willing
_____	_____
_____	_____
_____	_____
_____	_____
_____	_____
Names	*Names*
Needs Training	Needs Challenges

+

− ABILITY +

Delegate Like a Pro

Delegation is not a data dump of your entire unwanted, not hard to do, not so interesting tasks onto the head of another person. Rather, it is a carefully crafted process of defining what you want done, the specific end results you expect, and the process by which the other person can win at delivering it. To insure that the time you invest in delegating is well spent, use the following five-step process:

Step 1: Define the end results.

One of the most obvious oversights that managers make is failing to provide clarity about the end results they expect. Before you have a sit-down with one of your staff members, clarify in your own mind the dimensions of the assignment to be carried out. Ask yourself: *What are the specific conditions that, if met, will satisfy me?* It's a common mistake to assume that these conditions are implicit and that you don't need to make them explicit—you do. For example, say you are delegating a report to a subordinate:

Do you want your subordinate to do the research for the report and present you with his or her initial findings verbally or in writing before he or she creates the report?

Or...

Do you want him or her to do the research for the report and then write up a first draft, which he or she then shows you?

Or...

Do you want your subordinate to do the research, write the report, and then oversee production and distribution of the report, just checking in with you from time to time to make sure he or she is on the right track?

Step 2: Clarify the parameters.

Depending on the importance of the item delegated, and the willingness and ability of the person being delegated to, the degree of control and influence you exercise will vary. There are three basic types of delegation each allowing the staff member a varying degree of authority. Decide ahead of time which type best fits the task you are turning over:

Assignment: You tell the staff member what is to be done and how to do it.

Involvement: You tell the staff member what is to be done and determine together how to do it.

Empowerment: You tell the staff member the result to be accomplished and let him or her decide how to do it.

Hot Hint: It is important that you determine a time by which the delegated item will be completed. This can be wholly determined by you, by your staff, or by mutual agreement, depending on the degree of control and influence you have used in delegating this item.

Step 3: Come to a mutual agreement.

Once an item has been delegated, it's important to give the other person an opportunity to obtain some ownership over it. People usually have one of four responses to a delegated item:

- They accept the assignment, as is.
- They refuse the assignment, flat out.
- They accept the assignment, but want to negotiate the details of its delivery.
- They accept the assignment, but with certain conditions attached.

Don't automatically assume a delegated item has been accepted, as is. Instead, come to a mutual agreement on who will do what by when, and negotiate the details of delivery at the start. Having this degree of clarity on the front end will save scads of time and frustration on the back.

Hot Hint: When a staff member declines find out the reason(s) why. Is it a concern they have about himself or herself, you, or the assignment itself?

Step 4: Follow through and provide support.

Delegate, don't abdicate. When you transfer an item to a staff member, the responsibility for its completion still rests in your hands. To chart your staff's progress:

- Ask, *"How is it going?"*
- Set milestone meetings to review and discuss progress.
- Check in on quality control from time to time.
- Keep a visual display (charts and graphs) of the results produced.
- Ask staff members to occasionally account for their progress and problems.
- Be available to answer questions and provide feedback.
- Inform other people within the company of the staff member's responsibility.
- Periodically ask the staff member what support he or she needs from you.
- Provide the staff person with any ongoing information or necessary updates.

Step 5: Evaluate the success of the delegation.

It's de-motivating to put time and effort into an assignment, and then not receive any response (let alone appreciation or acknowledgment) for what has been accomplished. The last step in delegating like a pro is to recognize the results of the delegation/determine areas for improvement. This includes:

- Identifying the learning, growth, and development that occurred.
- Rewarding and/or thanking staff for their efforts and the results produced.
- Highlighting aspects of the job that could be improved in the future.
- Determining areas where your delegation skills could be improved in the future.

By taking this last step, you will not only help add to your staff the feeling of a job well done, but you will increase their willingness to take on delegated items in the future.

Polish Your Delegation Delivery

A customer comes up to the counter of a rental car company obviously upset. He informs the clerk, Monica, that he has been charged for an extra day because he returned his car two hours late. Monica, who has only been on the job for a few months, goes to the station manager, Peter, and explains the situation.

Monica: *I have a customer out here that is upset because he is being charged for an extra day. He says he is only two hours late and this does not warrant us charging him for a whole day. He also says he is a regular with us. What should I do?*

How would you rate the delegation effectiveness (good, fair, or poor) of the following various responses from Peter, Monica's manager?

Response #1:*Don't worry about it Monica, I'll handle it.*
I would rate this delegation as: __Good__Fair__Poor
Why?

___

Response #2: *Don't worry about it, Monica. This happens all the time. You can just go back, and tell him you spoke with your supervisor and he said the policy states that anything after the 56-minute grace period is charged at the full-day rate. If he gives you any problem, I will talk to him.*
I would rate this delegation as: __Good__Fair__Poor
Why?

___

Response #3: *Monica, you have been working here for a few months now and, from what I have seen, you are capable of handling this. Why don't you take a minute to think about the best way to resolve this situation? You know our policy, but, as you said, this is a regular customer. Use your own good judgment, and I will stand by any decision you make. Just keep in mind the goal here is to do what's right by both the customer and the company. How do you feel about that?*
I would rate this delegation as: __Good__Fair__Poor
Why?

___

And the Answer Is...

Response #1 is a *poor* example of delegation. By telling Monica that he will handle the situation, Peter is missing a major opportunity to train Monica to deal with this type of occurrence in the future. He is also encouraging her to bring all difficult problems to him, rather than learn to handle them herself.

Do: Take a long-term view of things and make the time now to train people in the ongoing skills they will need to get their jobs done over time.

Don't: Jump in and do it all yourself because it seems easier at the moment to do so. This type of short-term thinking leads to a time-management nightmare where you (and only you) can make things work.

Response #2 is a *fair* example of delegation. By explaining the policy, Peter is educating Monica and training her how in to handle these situations. He is also allowing her to communicate the decision to the customer, which will help her to deal with customer disagreements in the future. What Peter has not done is empower Monica to look beyond the policy and use her good judgment.

Do: Educate staff on the rules, regulations, policies, and procedures that apply to the item you are delegating, so that they are able to make appropriate decisions.

Don't: Minimize the creative power of your staff by limiting the discussion to the rules only. Real delegation is only possible with people who understand the policies and the circumstances in which they can be altered.

Response #3 is a *good* example of delegation. Peter has expressed his confidence in Monica with his words and, even more to the point, proven his faith by letting her make the call. He has highlighted the two most important points for her to consider (the customer is a regular and company policy) and has empowered Monica to weight these two factors against the ultimate goal. Finally, by asking her how she feels about the situation, he is checking to make sure that she is willing to take this delegation to make the decision.

Do: Give staff the biggest picture possible when you delegate an item. Having a big perspective helps them to make the best decisions and take the most appropriate actions towards the desired end.

Don't: Be afraid to delegate something that is a little over someone's head or presents a challenge to him or her. As long as you are there to support and back him or her up, a little stretch goes a long way.

Determine What to Delegate

Even though every manager knows what delegation is, few really understand how to make the most of it. When done well, delegation can be a win-win scenario for both parties—saving time on the assigner's part and building the abilities of the assignee. To begin with, you need to determine what items on your to-do list lend themselves to handing over. To determine what potential actions you could assign, check out the following:

Tasks That Are Routine

These are the everyday "C" items that you do to maintain your working environment. They are the routine, mundane actions that keep your office humming and usually involve errands, paperwork, and other low-priority tasks. Consider assigning these to new employees to check out their working habits and abilities. These can also be doled out to staff who may be between projects or find themselves with a bit of free time on their hands (as if!).

Tasks You Don't Have Time to Do

This is a group of items that are not necessarily routine, but of moderate priority. If more urgent or important matters are occupying your attention, pass these onto a capable subordinate who you know can handle the additional work.

Tasks That Involve Problem-Solving

There are some tasks before you that require a particular knowledge or skill to move forward. If one or more of your subordinates has the expertise or experience to tackle a particular problem, consider assigning them to it.

Tasks That Will Build an Individual's Capabilities

When properly managed, delegation can become a tool for training and developing your staff. Look and see what tasks you now do that you could hand over to a staff member that will provide a significant opportunity for his or her growth and development.

Tasks That Represent a Change in Job Emphasis

Over time, you may find that the emphasis of your job has changed, and you now have new responsibilities that require you to take on additional activities. As a matter of practicality you can delegate "old" activities associated with your previous job emphasis to make time and room for the new ones you need to take on.

Exercise

Review each of the five areas and determine one *real* item you would be willing and able to delegate.

A routine task I could delegate is

_____

A tasks I don't have time to do and could delegate is

_____

A task that involves problem-solving I could delegate is

_____

A task that will build someone's capability I could delegate is

A task that represents a change in job emphasis I could delegate is

---

Ask Before You Assign

Before you assign any task, be sure to answer the following questions:

- Is it crucial that I am the one to do this task, or is there someone else who has the expertise, experience, skill, or savvy needed to do it?
- Is there someone else I work with who would grow and develop as a result of my assigning this task?
- Is this an ongoing task that will become routine in the future?
- Am I willing to take and/or do I have the time (and energy) necessary to delegate this task effectively?

Take the Pulse of Your Procrastination

According to one study by Timothy Pychyl at the University of Ottawa, up to 70 percent of North Americans have a problem with procrastination! Are you one of them? Take the following quiz below to determine your current level of procrastination.

Thinking about your day-to-day work life, choose the most accurate answer for the following questions. Tally your score to see how big a role procrastination plays at work:

1 = Almost Never

2 = Once in a while

3 = Frequently

4 = All the time

1. I regularly put off starting tasks, projects, and activities I don't enjoy doing.____

2. Even when I have a specific deadline, I wait until the last minute to take action.____

3. When I have to make a tough decision, I put it off as long as possible.____

4. Even though I feel bad when I don't get started on an important task, this rarely motivates me to get going.____

5. I am regularly late for meetings and appointments.
____

6. I find myself needing to ask for time extensions on work due.____

7. I regularly say to myself, "I will do it tomorrow."
____

8. I have lost business or damaged relationships by putting things off.____

9. Even when I am excited about starting a new project, I have trouble initiating it.____

10. I can easily lose my focus and become distracted by trivial matters.____

Total score:____

10–15: Congratulations! Other than the normal procrastination here and there, you are not a chronic or problem procrastinator.

To improve your get-it-done muscle even more, determine several high-priority goals, and schedule a specific day and period of time to work on them.

16–25: You are not a serious procrastinator, but you could benefit from using a priority system to make you more effective and efficient. Resist the lure of the trivial by using a priority system based on achievement and importance, not crisis and time sensitivity.

26–32: Procrastination is having a negative impact on your work life and career. One reason may be that you feel overwhelmed with all the things you have on your plate. Try breaking your bigger projects into smaller tasks. This will help you take action more quickly and easily.

33–40: You have a serious case of procrastination. Evaluate the impact this is having on your professional accomplishments and relationships. Many serious procrastinators are distracted by technology. E-mail, voice mail, instant messaging, and the Internet are all wonderful tools, but, when they cause constant interruption, they make it almost impossible to focus at work. Draw a line by creating some technology-free times.

Give Yourself a Procrastination Inoculation

A recent study by Dr. Piers Steel, a professor at the University of Calgary, concluded that procrastination is on the rise. According to Steel's research, in 1978 about 15 percent of the population were considered moderate procrastinators. Today that number is up to 60 percent, a fourfold increase.

Another significant finding was that up to 95 percent of North Americans claim they procrastinate around work issues, costing businesses billions in lost revenue and productivity. Although procrastination is to some degree a natural phenomenon and can't be completely eradicated, utilizing the following strategies can beat it down:

Take Advantage of Your Power Hours

Are you an early riser who tackles your morning to-do list with all the gusto of a bear eating honey? Perhaps you're a night-owl and crank through your most pressing projects at 11:00 p.m.?

Either way, knowing and taking advantage of your natural energy patterns will help you steer clear of procrastination by using your power times to tackle the projects you find most challenging.

Use the Clout of Your Calendar

Do you have a task that has been lingering on your to-do list for days, weeks, or even (gulp) months? If so, use the clout of your calendar to move from inertia to action. Open your planner or PDA and schedule a specific date and time period when you promise yourself that you will work on that item—and that item only.

Decide on the Next Action

One reason people procrastinate is they feel intimidated by the task as it is currently stated and can't figure out what to do next. To overcome overwhelm, figure out the next smallest, easiest, and most comfortable action you could take to move forward. By breaking down the bigger, less-defined item into smaller, more specific chunks, you tell your mind "I can do this!"

Give Yourself Credit All Along the Way

The moment you take any action—no matter how small—give yourself credit. Don't wait until the entire to-do is complete before experiencing at least some degree of satisfaction and accomplishment.

Tackle the Hard Ones First

Almost everyone has more focus, energy, and attention available at the beginning of their workday than at the end. When you have to do a hard task, get it out of the way and do it first thing in the morning. This way it won't nag at you all day long.

Be Decisive

Putting off a decision about what to do with that piece of paper won't be any easier tomorrow than it is today. Train yourself to categorize every item that comes across your desk as something to do now, delegate, dump, or defer. Defer does not mean placing it back in the pile and pretending it does not exist. That is the pathway to procrastination. It means putting it in a dated tickler file, scheduling a time to do it, or moving it to a someday to-do list—where the guilt and stress of procrastination don't apply.

Chunk Down

Urban legend and Internet lore has it that on June 20, 1995, Dick Miller completed eating the last chunk of a 2,800-pound automobile. He started with two lug nuts and finished, five years later, by devouring the last of the clutch hosing. So, the next time you get stopped dead in your tracks by a colossal, gargantuan, oversized, almost-impossible-to-surmount project, remember to do what the mysterious Mr. Miller did, and chunk your endeavor down into confrontable, doable, bite-sized pieces.

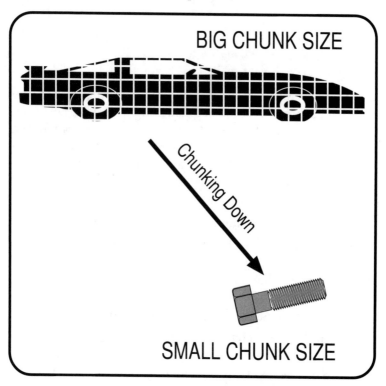

Thankfully, in the world of work, chunking down doesn't require eating metal (although some of your tasks may be just as difficult to swallow), but rather looking at your projects, goals, and more daunting tasks from a new perspective.Chunking down is about determining the actions you can quickly and easily take, without getting overwhelmed.

Traditional project management involves breaking a large project down into logical milestones. For example, if you had a goal to implement a company-wide classroom training on diversity in the workplace, your main objectives might include:

Time Management In An Instant

1. Form a task team to determine key learning objectives for the training.
2. Create a request for proposal (RFP) for potential vendors.
3. Select a vendor.
4. Create a master class schedule.
5. Conduct post-training assessment.

Although these steps represent a logical progression, all of these actions are fairly substantial and could seem overwhelming to implement—leading to procrastination. Upon closer examination, each of these milestones is composed of a string of mini-tasks. For example, the milestone *"select a vendor"* could be chunked down into the following series of smaller to-do's:

1. Develop list of accredited vendors to send the RFP to.
2. Send the RFP out to the potential vendor list.
3. Convene task team to review all proposals sent in by potential vendors.
4. Create a short list of three or four potential vendors.
5. Call references for vendors on the short list.
6. Invite vendors on the short list to make a presentation to the team.
7. Schedule vendor presentations to the task team.
8. Determine vendor of choice and negotiate contract details.

Even these mini-tasks could be further broken down into smaller chunks. For example *"develop a list of accredited vendors to send the RFP to"* could include:

1. Conduct web research on what vendors might be available.
2. Get suggested list of vendors from HR department.

3. Ask colleagues in another company who have implemented a similar training for potential vendors.

And so on.

The trick with chunking down is to learn to take the action you want to achieve and break it down into as many smaller steps as you need to in order to be able to easily confront getting it done—mentally, emotionally, and physically.

Exercise

Write down one project, goal, or task that you want to get done, but has become stalled or stuck in the mud.

_____

Now, chunk it down into as many mini-tasks as you can think of that seem doable. If the mini-task you have listed seems overwhelming, break it down into even smaller action items. When done, you should have a to-do list of actions you can take that will move you forward on your project but seem relatively easy to do. You know you have reached the right chunk size when you breathe a sigh a relief.

Mini task #1

_____

Mini task #2

_____

Mini task #3

_____

Mini task #4

_____

Mini task #5

_____

Mini task #6

_____

Mini task #7

_____

Mini task #8

_____

It's Time To Chunk Down When:

- You feel overwhelmed by the task.
- You have been procrastinating getting the item done.
- You have transferred the item five times in your calendar.
- The thought of doing the task makes you want to cry.

Assign Every Meeting a PAL

To make an immediate improvement in your meeting time management, use the PAL (purpose, agenda, and limits) method. Simple and straightforward, this system insures a basic level of meeting mindfulness that prevents wasted time and effort. Even regular meetings will benefit by applying the following PAL principle.

P = What is the Purpose of the meeting?

In his book *The 7 Habits of Highly Effective People*(Free Press, 2004), author Stephen Covey says to "begin with the end in mind." Before convening any meeting, take some time to write down a few sentences that articulate your overall objective for the get-together.

A good place to start is to think about what you hope will have happened by the *end* of the session. For example:

> *The task team will agree on the location and theme of this year's office holiday party.*

> *The sales group will be able to easily discuss our latest product with customers.*

> *The finance department will arrive at a decision about which vendor to hire to help with the office makeover.*

The more specific and concrete you make your meeting's purpose, the more focused your gathering will be and the greater your ability to evaluate your overall success.

A = Set a specific <u>A</u>genda.

Think of the stated agenda as the road map that will guide you through the meeting, keep you from veering off course, and avoid your getting distracted by the various goings on by the side of the road. A well-defined agenda lets all participants know what to expect from the meeting *and* what will be expected of them. In some cases you may want to develop the agenda in collaboration with other members of your company. In general, a well-rounded agenda includes:

- The intended purpose of the meeting.
- The date, start time, and finish time.
- The location.
- Specific objectives to be achieved.
- Topics to be discussed (and in what order).
- Any background information the participants need to know.
- Any other relevant information, such as dress code, pre-work, and so forth.

Time Management In An Instant

Here's an example of a sample agenda memo:

To: Sales Team
From: Bruce Buttermilk
Subject: Baseball Team Uniform Meeting

Date: January 27th
Location: International House of Pancakes
Times: 7:30 a.m. – 9:00 a.m.

Purpose: To agree on the baseball team uniform design for this year's softball tournament.

Agenda: Coffee, pancake breakfast, and socializing.
Introduction of new team members.
Review of last year's color scheme suggestions.
Presentation by the art department of sample team uniform drawings.
Discussion of pros and cons of various uniform designs.
Vote on uniform design.

L = Stick to a time Limit.

Meetings that start late and run over wreak havoc with everyone's schedule, and test their patience and goodwill. Every meeting you set up should have a stated start and finish time—which you stick to. If you discipline yourself and your co-workers to take your time limits seriously, your meetings promise to be more productive.

Hone the Habits of Meeting Management

A 2005 Microsoft Office Personal Productivity Challenge study of more than 38,000 people in 200 countries found that in the United States workers spend 5.5 hours a week in meetings, with 71 percent proclaiming that these meetings are unproductive. Who knew? What exactly makes these meetings time-wasters? Usually it's a combination of poor planning, poor execution, and poor follow-up. To add more gumption to your next gathering:

Assign Pre-work

If you want to raise the stakes for those attending, give the attendees something to think about or prepare prior to arrival. Among other things, you can ask them to read background information, come prepared with a suggested solution to a given problem, or show up ready to share a good story that illustrates the topic of the meeting. At a minimum, make sure everyone invited receives the agenda at least 24 hours before the meeting; this will at least get them mentally prepared to participate.

Invite the Right People

Deciding who to invite and who to leave out of a particular meeting may seem obvious, but how often has a decision been put off or a conclusion delayed because the right people (decision-makers, stakeholders, informed parties, experts, and so forth) were not in the room? In reviewing your purpose and agenda for the meeting, make an initial list of who you think should be invited, and then ask a colleague or two for their two cents before you finalize the invites.

Don't Delay

Right off the bat, you can set the mood for the meeting by starting on time. This honors those who showed up promptly and lets the tardy know that you mean what you say when it comes to time lines.

Hot Hint: When people do come in late, don't scowl at them as though they have the plague. Instead welcome them politely. Over time you will set an example for being punctual and polite—and you will train your co-workers to act accordingly.

Conduct Check-Ins

If you have a meeting that lasts more than a few hours, check in every once and a while to insure that you're on track. Go around the room and ask each participant to give you their feedback as to how they think the meeting is progressing. Try and avoid generalizations (such as fine, good, okay, and not great) by asking people to provide specific evaluations. For example:

"Fine." vs. "We seem to be covering a lot of ground."

"Okay." vs. "We don't seem to be sticking to our time line very well."

The more unambiguous the responses, the better the chance of adjusting your course when necessary. Be sure to check in with the more senior people in the group last. This prevents the other participants from having to offer an opinion counter to that of their boss, or their bosses' boss.

Assign Action Items
All Along the Way

A meeting without action items is like matzo-ball soup without the matzo balls. Don't move on from a significant discussion point within a meeting without flagging potential action items (no matter how small) and assigning them to group members. Doling out tasks that make their way to the surface of the conversation during the meeting will prevent a delay of game in getting things done down the road.

Avoid a Rush to Judgment

Beware of letting end-of-meeting madness push everyone into a "let's just make a decision already, end the suffering, be done with this meeting, and get back to our real jobs" mentality. This leads to a poor decision that everyone buys into or a good decision that no one supports. It's far better to schedule a follow-up meeting to conclude the matter completely.

Ponder Your Process

It's always a good idea to spend a few minutes at the end of every meeting reviewing the success of the process itself. Asking the group to describe what worked well about the meeting, and what actions could be taken the next time to improve, sets the stage for future enhancements.

Close With Closure

Just as you started on time, end on time. Always leave a few minutes for reviewing the actions assigned during the meeting and verifying the next meeting time. Minutes, including agreed upon to-do's, should be sent out within a few days.

Mind Your Meeting Minutes

Don't underestimate the importance of being able to go back and look up minutes from previous meetings. They can be a useful source for verifying agreements made, decisions rendered, and actions committed to. To get the facts at your fingertips easily and quickly, file all meeting minutes by date.

Promote Participation in Meetings

Nothing can slow down the momentum of a meeting and waste time the way unengaged, uncooperative, or uninterested participants can. Knowing how to deal with these difficult-to-please participants will greatly increase your meeting's effectiveness.

Bored and Showing It

Participants who are bored can bring down the mood of a meeting like a lead balloon. Their refusal to participate leaves you doing all the work. Instead of wading through the molasses of their disinterest, save time—and energy—by doing a fun exercise that shakes the group out of their doldrums.

Pose a question that relates to the agenda and ask everyone to write down their answer. Go around the room and have everyone share what they came up with.

Create a five-question quiz, relevant to the agenda, that tests everyone's knowledge of the subject at hand. Have individuals write down their answers on a piece of paper, and then discuss the correct answers.

Meeting Hogs

These are the people that know the answer to everything and take issue with anything anyone else says. Left unchecked, they can turn a lively group of participants into a quiet crowd of suppressed attendees. To rein them in, make it clear that you are interested in hearing from everyone in the group by saying, *"I appreciate you sharing your opinion about this, and now I'd like to hear what other people have to say."*

Break out into discussion groups so the participants can share their ideas and opinions in a smaller, "safer" environment. Have a member from each group report on what happened. This technique is also good for dealing with shy people who feel uncomfortable speaking in front of the whole group.

Angry and Upset

Occasionally a few individuals (or even your whole group) will be up in arms about a particularly hot agenda item. To keep the session from turning into a time-wasting complain-a-thon, express empathy for the emotion but suggest that the time in the meeting would best be served by focusing on solutions. Try saying, *"I understand that this is upsetting and I can see why you are angry, but I want us to spend our time figuring out how we are going to solve this problem, not just complain about it."*

Shy and Timid

It is not unusual for people with great ideas to feel uncomfortable sharing them in a big group. Rather than miss out on their valuable input, encourage quieter members to participate by saying, *"I haven't heard much from you this afternoon. Is there anything you'd like to add?"*

Strengthen Your Meeting Facilitation Skills

According to a 2005 study on meetings published in the *Journal of Applied Psychology,* goal-oriented staff report that their job satisfaction goes down as the number of meetings they attend goes up! Don't just sit back and play the passive part of monitor for the meetings you chair. Instead, take on the proactive role of facilitator by doing the following:

Direct the Discussion

Rather than allowing the meeting to veer off into a variety of different directions—based on individual agendas and random streams of consciousness—keep the group focused and on track by gently guiding them towards the stated purpose and agenda of the meeting. If the discussion wanders, try saying:

"We have gotten a bit off the topic; let's go back to the main point."

"I think we should stay focused on...."

"That's a good point, but one that should probably be discussed in a separate meeting."

Model Listening

As the facilitator, you set the tone for the meetings you lead. Avoid distracted behaviors such as answering your cell phone, text messaging, checking your e-mail, and so on. Instead, listen carefully to what is being said, and show interest by taking notes, paraphrasing, and nodding. This creates a mood of respect and attention that everyone can emulate. Remember: The more focus people bring to a meeting, the faster it goes.

Encourage Participation

If people feel that they have made a valuable contribution to a meeting, they are less likely to think that their time was wasted. Here are some ways you can encourage participation and give everyone a chance to have his or her say:

- Graciously suggest that a long-winded speaker, who is dominating the group discussion, get to the heart of his or her point so that others have time to express their opinions as well. Say something along the lines of, "*Rosemary, in order to give other people a chance to speak, I'd appreciate it if you could give us the bottom line of the point you're making.*" This will usually do the trick.

- Set a two-minute time limit per person for the sharing of ideas and feedback.

- Ask the group a question and go around the room requesting a response from each person.

- Offer to answer excessive and/or off-point questions that are taking up the group's time after the meeting.

Recap the Results

To reaffirm the value of the meeting (and the time invested) summarize the next steps, decisions, and accomplishments that came out of the session before adjourning.

Establish Ground Rules

Ground rules set out a common code of conduct and help keep unproductive meeting behavior to a minimum. Of course, different ground rules are appropriate for different groups and situations, but some of the more common ones include:

- Don't interrupt when someone else is talking.
- Critique the idea, not the person.
- Be back from the breaks on time.
- Don't answer cell phones when in the session.

Hot Hint: Once ground rules are created (and agreed to) they should be clearly posted during the session. If someone breaks one, don't be afraid to tactfully point it out.

Step Back and Problem Solve

Contrary to the belief (popular among high achievers and productivity superstars) that it's better to fire first and aim second, taking just a small amount of time on the front end to reflect on a problem can save frustration and effort on the back end. To get things done, the right way, the first time, try the following quick and easy actions:

Find the Real Cause of the Problem

Is the problem you have identified the real one or just a sign of a deeper issue? Coming up with solutions that address the symptoms of a problem may be a good interim step, but, if you don't get to the heart of what's not working, more effort will be required down the road. A good way to get at the cause of the perceived problem is to ask yourself and your co-workers, "*Why does this problem really exist?*" Keep asking that question until you get to what you consider to be the essential cause.

For example, if the initial problem was stated as "*The quality of our responses to incoming phone calls has deteriorated.*" Reflection and discussion might reveal that "*our staff needs training on the new telephone system.*" Even further inquiry might make it clear that the underlying reason is "*We can't take staff off the phone long enough to put them through the training program!*"

Hot Hint: Often, when you are very familiar with a problem or the problem has been around for a long time, there is a tendency to assume, rather than verify, the underlying causes.

Brainstorm Possible Solutions

The whole idea behind brainstorming is to encourage as many ideas as possible to be put forth. Sometimes, an idea that seems crazy and far-fetched can become the initiative and inspiration that leads to a stellar solution. For example, if the cause of the problem is "*we cannot take staff off the phones long enough to get them trained*" some possible solutions might include:

Design a shorter phone training that fits into our shift schedule.

Take the current four-hour training and break it down into four, one-hour modules.

Pay staff to come in on their off time to attend the training.

Turn the live training into an online program with home-study manuals.

Choose a Viable Solution

After listing a few possible solutions, it will become obvious which ones are the most practical. Before leaping head first into a solution consider:

- The short-term impact of the solution.
- The long-term impact of the solution.
- The relative cost of implementing the solution.
- The availability of resources needed to implement the solution.
- The commitment and support of management to implement the solution.
- The chances that the solution will create a new problem(s).

Forecast the Success of a Solution

If you're thinking about implementing a change (personal or business, big or small), you can avoid the wasted time of a less-than-viable decision by applying the problem-solving tool of Force Field Analysis. In short, Force Field Analysis is a four-step process that helps you objectively assess the barriers to and drivers towards a successful solution. In order for any change to take hold, the driving forces (those pushing for the change) must be greater than the hindering forces (those pushing against the change). The four steps in the process are:

Step 1: Write down the specific proposed change/solution in the center of the worksheet.

Step 2: In the left-hand column list all the forces that you can think of that are hindering or pushing *against* the proposed change/solution.

Step 3: In the right-hand column list all the forces that you can think of that are supporting or pushing *for* the proposed change/solution.

Step 4: Using a scale of 1–10 (1 = weak and 10 = strong) score the relative strength of each of the forces. Do this for both columns.

Here's an example: Imagine you are considering *hiring a full-time Web-marketing expert* to do a search-engine campaign for your small business. Your worksheet might look this way:

FORCE FIELD ANALYSIS WORKSHEET

SCORE 1 - 10	DRIVING FORCES	PROPOSED CHANGE	HINDERING FORCES	SCORE 1 - 10
8	Increased sales		Short-term cost	6
4	Extra person will lighten load		Learning curve to understand business	3
3	Comprehensive and organized approach	Hire a full-time Web-marketing expert	Extra person will crowd current office	5
3	Save on outsourcing costs over time		Busy buying season is over. Delay until next year	4
2	Website always current			

Looking at the worksheet, this decision will more than likely be successful because the driving forces outweigh the hindering forces—by two points. If the opposite were true, and the hindering forces were greater than the driving forces, the chances of success would be reduced.

Exercise

Using the following blank worksheet, choose a change/solution you are thinking of making and work through the four steps of Force Field Analysis to see if it's worth investing your time and energy.

FORCE FIELD ANALYSIS WORKSHEET

SCORE 1 - 10	DRIVING FORCES	PROPOSED CHANGE	HINDERING FORCES	SCORE 1 - 10

Hot Hint: If the results of your analysis show a project where the numbers don't make sense, but the change is still one you want to make, brainstorm ways you could reduce the strength of the forces hindering the project and increase the forces of the ones driving it.

Take a Real Vacation

Have you ever noticed that stories about life in the very far-off future often present a vision where leisure and vacations are the rule and hard work the exception? In reality, for all the talk about technology and its impact on time off, most people don't really know how to get away and leave it all behind.

A recent survey by the recruiting firm Hudson found that more than half of American workers fail to take all their vacation days. Thirty percent say they use less than half their allotted time, and 20 percent take only a few days instead of a week or two. Another survey by OfficeTeam found that 76 percent of executives attend to office duties several times while on vacation, and 33 percent conduct business every day. One reason so many people find it difficult to disconnect is a lack of planning to leave. To make the most of your vacation:

Spread the Word

Contact clients, co-workers, and vendors with the dates you will be gone and a point person they can contact in your absence. Be sure to leave this information on your voice mail and e-mail.

Delegate Decisions

Authorize a co-worker you have confidence in to make decisions on your behalf while you're gone. Make sure and leave any important information your colleagues may need readily available and easily accessible on your desk.

Limit Contact

If you have to check in with your office, schedule specific days and times when you are going to make contact and stick to it. If your coworkers know that you are not *on call,* the chances of you being interrupted by office issues are greatly reduced.

Plan Ahead

If practical, schedule your vacation during a slower period at work and let your manager know as soon as possible, so he or she can plan for your absence.

Unplug

Consider leaving your computer at home. If you need access to e-mail or the Internet, use the business center at your hotel.

Prepare for Return

To put your mind at ease about all the work you will have to do upon returning, create a to-do list before you go of items you will need to handle within your first few days back.

Create Closure

Get ready to go a few weeks before you leave by closing any open items that could come back to haunt you while you are away. This includes paying bills, updating reports, sending off proposals and invoices, and cleaning off your desk so it's neat and tidy for your return.

46

Try a Staycation

Are you in desperate need of some time away from the office but, for whatever ever reason, just can't jet off to France, cruise to Hawaii, or take a cross-country car trip any time soon? No worries. Try the latest creation of the overwhelmed and overscheduled: Take a *staycation,* a new buzzword that means a vacation you take from the comfort of your own home. To make the most of your home grown break from the office:

Avoid Errand Creep

Don't end up doing so many things around the house—replacing the lightbulbs, cleaning out the garage, fixing the front door, and so forth—that you miss taking the time you need to just chill. If you have a few closets you really want to clean out, schedule a specific day and time to do them.

Keep Friends at Bay

Unless you want a major part of your staycation to be visiting with friends, don't over-schedule lunches, dinners, and get-togethers. You want the space (and freedom) to be spontaneous.

Set Goals

Think about what you want to accomplish on your staycation. Is there a book you have been dying to read? A whole slew of movies you want to catch up on? Romantic time you want to spend with your spouse? A new exhibit at the zoo to take the kids to? Time to think through your long-term goals? Naps? Whatever objectives you set, let them dictate the organization of your time off.

Block Out Check-In Times

Just as you would with a regular getaway vacation, set up specific times when you are going to check in with the office, and stick to them. Don't let the proximity of work lure you away from your stay-at-home holiday.

Create a Budget

Although you won't have the expenses of leaving home, you will want to consider how much your staycation activities will cost. If you plan on eating out more, spending one or two nights at a local hotel, or starting a project that requires investment, plan a budget.

Stay Overnight

If your staycation is a week or longer, consider spending one or two nights at a local hotel. Just getting away for a night can feel exotic and fun (not to mention romantic, if you go with your significant other).

Become a Tourist

You know that old joke about how most New Yorkers have never been to the Statue of Liberty? Buy a guidebook on the area you live in, and read through it for things you might like to do. Take a guided tour, helicopter ride, or boat trip.

Visit a Day Spa

Just because you're not staying at a five-star resort with a world-class spa does not mean you can't get scrubbed, rubbed, and pampered! Check out a day spa in your area, and set up a treatment or two. If you really want to splurge, go for broke and do a full-day package.

Hire Some Help

Want a break from cooking and cleaning for your week off? Hire someone else to do it. Order in, or hire a day maid, a driver, a cook, or any number of other helpers who can give you a life of leisure—at least for a few days.

Do Something Different

One of the advantages of a traditional vacation is that it puts you in a different environment, where the opportunity to try something new is greater than usual. There is no reason you can't apply this same idea to your staycation. Check out your local scene for activities that you might not normally do but that sound fun.

Do Nothing

Never underestimate the value of waking up when you want to and doing whatever you want, whenever you want, all day long. Don't feel that your staycation has to produce any tangible results— it doesn't. Just getting renewed and refreshed is reward enough.

47

Stay Sane Getting Back From Vacation

For most people the excitement of going on vacation is equaled only by the stress they feel a few days before getting back to work. Returning to the office can often wipe out (within hours) all the relaxation built up over a week on Waikiki. Worry not. With a little bit of organizing you can avoid the back-from-vacation blues and insure that the benefits of your vacation are felt long after your plane has touched down on the tarmac.

Catch Up First

Before the raging river of your to-do list carries you away, begin by catching up with your co-workers. Penelope Trunk, author of *Brazen Careerist* (Business Press, 2007), says that burying your head in paperwork the minute you hit your office and griping to everyone about how overwhelmed you are makes you look too inefficient to even take a vacation. Instead, Trunk says the best strategy is take a walk around the office. "Share about your vacation and ask people how they are doing and what's been going on. This gives them a chance to let you know about something they may have wanted to talk with you about, but didn't feel comfortable hitting you with your first day back," she says.

Don't Clutter Up Your Calendar

David Allen, author of *Ready For Anything* (Penguin, 2004), says businesspeople misjudge the amount of time it will take to get caught up. "It takes an hour a day on average for the typical professional to gather, process and organize all their inputs," says Allen. "Think about how many days you will be away and then assign an hour for each day. If you're gone for two weeks, that's two days at least." Allen suggests keeping a relatively clear calendar for those first few days back.

Hot Hint: Come home a day early or add an extra day to the back end of your vacation. This will provide a transition time for unpacking and getting settled.

Remember the 80/20 Rule

While you were away, tons of to-do's (electronic and otherwise) will have made their way into your in-box, but not all of these warrant immediate action. "Most people want to come running in and start going through all their emails," says Dr. Pamela Dodd, author of *The 25 Best Time Management Tools & Techniques* (Peak Performance Press, 2005). Instead, she suggests people determine the most important 20 percent of the open items to get done, which will produce 80 percent of the results in terms of getting back to work smoothly.

Make Changes

Vacations not only give you a much-needed break from the stresses of work, but they also provide an opportunity to step back and get some perspective on your life. "Vacations give you thinking space," says Trunk, "but you can't leverage that if you go back to your desk and do exactly the same thing." She says people need to think about how they are going to change to accommodate what they discovered while away. For example, if your vacation sparked a yearning to spend more time on your photography, when you get back, try to stop booking meetings on Fridays after 3:00. Doing so could allow you to leave a bit early and spend the later part of the afternoon pursing your hobby.

Use Your Conference Time Wisely

Attending a conference can be entertaining and educational, and offer unique opportunities for networking with others in your industry—or it can be a dreary, dull, and disappointing waste of time. To make the most of any business or industry conference you attend, prepare ahead, use your time on site wisely, and plan on post-conference follow-up.

Pre-conference

Choose your sessions early. Instead of making a last-minute, seat-of-the-pants decision on what sessions to attend over coffee and croissants the morning of, take the time to review the conference agenda and sessions well in advance. This gives you time to check out the Websites of various presenters, research best recommendations from colleagues, and put together a more well-rounded agenda. To get the most bang for your buck when choosing tracks, give strong consideration to sessions that:

- Offer a practical application of the topic being discussed.
- Expand your current knowledge and skill set.
- Fall outside your comfort zone, and stretch you to learn something new and/or challenging.
- Are presented by someone you admire or have wanted to hear speak for a long time.

Set up appointments in advance. Do some research on which vendors, colleagues, and potential customers may be attending the same conference and set up appointments now, to meet with them later. Many people wait and hope to casually contact the person at the conference. Though this type of spontaneous get together does occur, some opportunities should not be left to chance.

Prepare an elevator speech. You will be asked this one question dozens (if not hundreds) of times as you stand in line for the breakfast buffet, settle into your seat for a session, and sip coffee on a break: *What do you do?*

Having a pithy and punchy description of your work (project, goal or dream, and so forth) will make networking, and standing around in line, more productive. The key is to develop a snappy and interesting 30-second description (elevator speech) of what you do.

Plan to stay at the conference hotel. Even super-duper large conference hotels sometimes book up in advance. As soon as you know you want to attend a conference, book a room at the hosting hotel, or one as close as possible to the location where the events will be held. Staying at the conference hotel will save you time in the morning (your commute will be in an elevator, not on a congested roadway). Likewise, taking breaks, making phone calls, and checking e-mail is a more comfortable and convenient in the privacy of your own room, just a few floors above.

At the Conference

Have a backup plan. If, fifteen minutes into your carefully chosen session, your eyes start to roll up into the back of your head, have a backup plan in mind.

Hot Hint: Sit at the back of the room, near the door, or on an aisle. This way you can make your exit as unobtrusively as possible.

Map out where you are going. Study the event map and figure out, at the beginning of each day, the route you will follow to get to each session. This will save you having to sprint through corridors, run over roads, and dash down tunnels in order to be on time. Remember to leave extra time for slow elevators and side conversations.

Manage your energy. Conferences are notorious for testing the intestinal fortitude of even the strongest among us. To avoid falling asleep a few minutes into your first afternoon session, forego the Chocolate Decadence Cheesecake Fudge Brownie a la Mode at lunch.

Hot Hint: Really listening hour after hour, and day after day, takes more energy than you realize. To make sure you have the stamina to focus on what you are learning, get enough sleep and be mindful of your alcohol intake at the evening events. A hangover will most certainly not improve you concentration.

Maximize networking. Set a goal to meet at least one new person each day of the conference. The more you participate in the sessions and activities offered, the more value you will take away. Whenever practical, attend the conference with a colleague or co-worker. By attending different sessions, you can swap what you learned and, in effect, both have attended two sessions at the same time. Now that's time management in an instant!

Post-conference

Schedule a post-conference follow-up. The business cards you gathered at the conference are so exciting when you first get them that they seem to burn a hole in your pocket! But back at the office, those same cards, amidst all the things you now have to catch up on, can feel as if they're a rock weighing you down. Within a few days of the conference (or on the plane ride home) make a to-do list of the people you need to follow up with and actions you want to take. Transfer all relative information from the brochures and business cards to the list, open up your calendar, and commit to a specific date and time within the next week to process the items on the list.

Make the Most of an Off-Site

If you or your team needs some concentrated time to sort out a strategy, solve a big problem, or step back and innovate, an off-site may be just what the doctor ordered. Getting away from the office, and the usual interruptions, can revive your enthusiasm for a business or project, and rev up your focus. To make the most of your time away:

Take 1 to 5 Days Away

If possible, stay for longer than a day. Even though you save money by eliminating overnight accommodations, you miss out on the opportunity to socialize and informally discuss work-related issues in the evening.

Go Easy on the PowerPoint

Although certain data is no doubt important to communicate, back-to-back PowerPoint presentations and endless ramblings in a half-lighted room invite drowsiness—especially after lunch! Instead, create an agenda that incorporates group exercises, discussion, role-plays, hands-on working sessions, demonstrations, and interesting outside speakers.

Leave Some Breathing Room

A tightly packed schedule with no downtime leads to information overload and off-site burnout. Don't jam each day so full of activities that attendees never get a chance to catch their breath and reflect on what's being discussed.

Build in Flexibility

Don't be so tied to an agenda or time line that a hot, heavy, and important discussion gets shelved, just so that you can stay on schedule. The point of the retreat is to draw people in and get them to think, act, and participate in new ways.

Play

Though you want your off-site to be productive, you don't want it to be a grind. Setting up activities for play is an important part of the package. Ideas include a golf outing, dinner at a popular restaurant, a visit to a museum, theater tickets, and a spa treatment.

Off-Site Checklist

Here are a few things to consider to make your off-site a success before you even arrive:

- What is the purpose/theme of the off-site?
- Given the purpose, who should be invited?
- Who will select the site, make the arrangements, and coordinate with site management?
- What kind of "welcome" packet do you want the attendees to receive on arrival?
- Do you need audiovisual equipment? If so, who will be responsible for this?
- Who is your contact person at the site? Is this the person that any deliveries should be addressed to?

- Will you have any presentations during lunch or dinner? If so, is the catering department aware of your plans?
- Do you want organized entertainment in the evenings? What will it be, and who will organize it?
- What time is staff expected to arrive? Do they need driving directions? Is a meal being served upon arrival? Are you offering vegetarian food to those who need it?
- Once at the site, who will be responsible for overseeing arrivals, room allocation, and registration?
- How do you want to begin and end the off-site?

Clean Out Your File Drawer

Before you embark on the exciting task of creating a new super-organized filing system, you must tackle the dreaded task of cleaning out the old one. Although it may feel daunting to plod through the dusty memos of yesteryear, it can be uplifting to find forgotten (but important) bits and pieces, and energizing to throw away all that unnecessary paper!

Working from front to back, start with one file and as you examine the contents inside ask yourself:

- ***"Are there any actions I need to take on this?"*** If seeing the contents of the file sparks any actions you need to take, make a note of them on your to-do list and/or schedule a time to get them done. For example: a memo from a senior executive in your company requesting ideas on a new product launch, information on a potential new customer account, a brochure for an upcoming conference, and so forth. If you need to keep the data in the file around until you complete the action item, then keep it either in a file or in your in-box. If not, then throw it out and use the to-do list as your tickler to get it done.

- *"Do I need to keep this for tax or legal purposes?"* Though the item may be taking up space in your system, if you need to keep it for legal or tax purposes, clearly label it (for easy retrieval down the road) and then re-file. This category can include papers you may need for an audit, old contracts that apply to current vendor relationships, invoices, expense records, and other items not duplicated elsewhere. If you are not sure, keep it until you are *certain* that it is safe to discard.

- *"Is this recent reference material?"* Out-of-date journals, old brochures from distant conventions, and invitations to networking events long passed have no place in your current filing system. Dump them immediately! Other reference items such as articles, brochures, course notes, and seminar workbooks that are still of use now or in the near future should be kept.

- *"Will I ever need this again—really?"* Don't fall into the trap of saving something just because there is a small chance that someday, in some way, somehow, you may need it. Instead ask yourself if you can think of a specific (and realistic) situation in which this document might be useful or needed. If not, send it to the big wastepaper basket in the sky.

Hot Hint: When all else fails ask yourself *"What is the worst possible thing that would happen if I threw this away?"* If you can live with the answer, toss it.

> ### Scan It
> The recent introduction of small, multi-sheet scanners makes it easier than ever to scan multi-page documents quickly that you still want to keep, but not as a hard copy in your files.

Process Your Desktop In-Box

Long, long ago, at the start of the personal computer age, media pundits and high-tech hipsters proffered that technology would pretty much eliminate paperwork. Ha! One glance around the average corporate cubicle or home office reveals towering piles of paper stuffed in overflowing in-boxes.

To tame the paper tiger, go through your in-box one piece of paper at a time. Start from the top of the pile, and make a decision about what your next action is going to be for each item. How do you want to handle each item, according to the following categories?

Now Paperwork

This is anything that requires your immediate attention (for example, items for signature, urgent memos, time-limited to-do's, and so forth). If you can deal with it in two to five minutes, do it on the spot; you'll get a warm and tingly feeling when you only have to handle that piece of paper once. On the other hand, if the item requires more time to process (10 minutes or longer) schedule a specific time and day when you can do it, within the next two days. This prevents you from forgetting—and suffering the consequences of not handling a time-sensitive item.

Later Paperwork

This are the items that you intend to take action on, but that don't require the immediate attention of the "now" category. They may include invoices, bills, inquiries, brochures, and so on. This group also includes items you are waiting for more information on to process. In order to avoid a plethora of "later" papers turning your in-box into the Leaning Tower of Pisa, place these items in a second in-box or file folder marked "In Process" and review them once a week, moving as many to the "now" pile as possible.

Hot Hint: It can really help to move these things along if you also add them to your daily, weekly, or monthly to-do list as appropriate.

Reference Paperwork

You don't need to take any specific action on these items, though you may want to reference the material down the road. (For example, at tax time you will need all your receipts from the year readily available.) Place items that fall into this category, clearly labeled, in your filing system.

Choose Your Window

You can spend two minutes, two hours, or two days processing the items in your in-box. In order to be the most efficient, decide ahead of time which window of time you plan on spending in a particular processing session:

The two-minute window: Pick one item from your in-box that requires only one quick step to process and finish it.

The good five minutes: Some items can't be done in a nano-second but are only a few steps away from completion (for example, putting the brochure in the envelope, addressing it, and putting it through the postage machine). The next time you find yourself with a spare five minutes (it could happen!), pick one of these items and do it.

The hour purge: If you have several hefty items in your box that will take multiple steps to complete and that require research, plan on this longer concentrated window of time to get them done.

The dedicated day: If you have spring cleaning fever, your in-box is a total disaster, or you just have a whole lot of stuff piled up, consider setting aside a day (even a Saturday) to just plow through and process it all.

Reorganize Your Filing System

From the outside all file drawers look neat and organized, but, when you open them, the ugly truth is revealed. If your system is a muddled mess, you are probably in need of some R&R—re-labeling and reorganizing. Before you begin, gather together the following supplies:

> Hanging file folders (legal or letter, with plastic attachable tabs).
>
> Manila files (legal or letter, 1/3 or 1/5 cut).
>
> Adhesive labels (white or clear).
>
> Black marking pen.
>
> Label maker (optional).

Supplies in hand, start by making a list of the broad categories you will need. These categories form the core structure of your system and will be used to label your hanging folders. Common categories include:

- Clients.
- Conferences.
- Contracts.
- Finances.
- Insurance.
- Legal.
- Office Equipment.

- Projects.
- Research.
- Travel.

Once you have a complete list, stop, make a hanging file label for each category, and insert it in the plastic holder. When attached to the folder, the holders sit above the tops of all other files, and can always be easily seen and accessed. Place the labeled hanging folders in your filing system. Depending on your preference, you can either arrange them alphabetically, or place those more frequently used towards the front.

Next, sort each of your main categories into sub-categories to be used in labeling your file folders. For example, "Clients" might be broken down one file for each individual account; "Finances" may contain a folder for expense reports, invoices, 401(k), and so forth; and "Office Equipment" might involve a separate manila folder for each individual item such as your computer, printer, phone, and copier.

Hot Hint: You may want to sub-divide your sub-categories. How far down you break each category depends on the level you need to easily store paperwork and quickly find the file. For example, your "Invoice" folder (found in the "Finances" file) might lend itself to be further broken down into several folders including "Client Invoices," "Contractor Invoices," and "Vendor Invoices."

Now the exciting part: Once you have the sub-category list complete, label each manila folder and place it behind the appropriate broad category hanging file.

Sort the manila folders in each category alphabetically to make finding them as easy as possible.

Choose Your Words Carefully

When creating a filing system choose words that have the most meaning to you. For example, are you more likely to look for the file that says:

Finances or money?

Car or automobile?

Clients or accounts?

Travel or trips?

Research or reference?

The point of a filing system is to be able to quickly and easily retrieve items you need, not just stockpile paperwork. Labeling items in a way that is the most natural to how you think and talk will make this easier.

Sort Your Stuff

Stuff—it's everywhere. Pencil cups overflowing, cabinets filled to the max, and paperwork piled a mile high. Everyone needs their business bits and pieces, but, taken to an extreme, out-of-control stuff becomes clutter. And clutter saps your energy and slows you down. If your clutter-clearing efforts have fallen on hard times, don't despair. Here is an easy process to sort out your stuff and reclaim your space—one drawer at a time.

Choose a Limited Area to Work On

Assuming you don't have an entire day to dedicate to de-cluttering your office, choose a single stuff sorting area to work on. Be sure to allot an adequate amount of time so that you can finish what you start. For example: Your whole desk needs cleaning out, but you only have 30 minutes, so you are going to start with your two top drawers.

Do a "T" Scan

Moving in a logical direction (right to left, top to bottom, front to back), scan the stuff in front of you. As you come across each item, assign it a category and act accordingly.

- **Trash.** This is an item that no longer works, you no longer need, or you no longer like. It has outlived its usefulness and is ready to make the journey from your office to the wastebasket. *Action: Throw this out now! If the item is still in good working shape, put it in a box to be given to charity.*

- **Treasure.** This is an item you need, you like, and/or you use. It belongs exactly where it is. *Action: Don't do a thing. Leave it as it and be glad you found it.*

Hot Hint: If the item is one you want, but it needs to be repaired, ask yourself if it's worth the time and effort to fix the item, or if it would be better to replace it. If the answer is to repair it, schedule a specific time to take care of it within the next week.

- **Transfer.** This is an item that you want to keep but that does not belong in the location where you found it. *Action: Put the item in a box for transfer to its proper place when the sorting session is over.*

- **Temptation.** This is an item that you feel conflicted over. Part of you wants to keep it, and part of you is not sure you will ever use it. To help decide ask yourself:
  - Do I have more than one of these?
  - How useful will this really be in the future?
  - When was the last time I used this?
  - Is this something I need to keep for legal reasons?
  - What is the worst thing that could happen if I get rid of this?

Action: Make a decision now. For better or worse, choose a course of action on this item and bring it to closure.

Organize the Items

This is the part of the sorting session where you begin to think of plastic as the most magical thing every invented. Using a variety of drawer, desk, and cabinet organizers, rearrange your "treasures" so they can be easily seen and accessed.

Now step back, breathe deeply, and declare this area a clutter-free zone!

Manage Outgoing Calls

Even though e-mail is beginning to outpace the phone as the favored means of communication, most people still spend a good deal of time yakking on the wire. The following tips will help you save time by managing your outgoing calls.

Bundle Your Calls

Whenever practical, set aside a specific time for making all of your phone calls in one sitting. By grouping them together, you avoid the switching back and forth between tasks that break your workflow and concentration.

Hot Hint: On your planner or PDA, list your phone calls at the bottom of the page. This way they're always grouped together and easy to find.

Prepare an Agenda

Make a list of the specific items you want to cover on the call, and keep it in front of you. By thinking things through ahead of time, you can more easily stay focused and keep from veering off track (or having to call back with a forgotten item).

Call Early

If you have been playing telephone tag with someone, try calling him or her at the office between 7:30 a.m. and 9:30 a.m. (his or her local time).

Ask if He or She Is Available

Instead of just jumping in, let the other person know who is calling and ask, "*Is this is a good time to talk?*" If he or she says yes, you will have his or her full attention. If not, schedule a specific date and time when you can reconnect.

Leave Concise Messages

If you reach voice mail leave your name, a *brief* description of why you are calling, and the number where you can be reached (even if you think he or she has it). To cut down on telephone tag, offer specific times when you can be reached.

Use a Headset

It's not a good idea to work on other projects when you're on the phone, though a headset will free you up to take notes or look up pertinent information.

Hot Hint: Have another task close at hand that you can work on when you are put on hold for a long time.

Provide Alternate Phone Numbers

Telephone tag is a frustrating waste of time for both parties. You can shortcut a message marathon by giving your tag-mate several phone numbers where you can be reached and at what times.

Control Incoming Calls

Whereas you have a lot of control over the calls you make, you have decidedly less over those you receive. Your phone rings whether it's a convenient time for you or not. Managing your incoming calls means learning to minimize telephone interruptions and take back control of your time:

Set Up a Callback

If it's not a good time for you to talk, instead of saying, *"I can't talk right now; call me back,"* stop telephone tag in its tracks by suggesting you set up a specific time to talk later.

Cut to the Chase

If you're short on time and the caller is long on chit chat, help him or her get to the point by explaining that you are on a deadline, about to leave for a meeting, or in the middle of project. To speed things along ask:

> *What can I do for you?*
> *How can I help with this?*
> *What specifically do you need?*

Wrap It Up

If you need to get off the call and the other person shows no signs of signing off, you can move things along by reiterating action steps. For example: *"It's been good talking to you. I will follow up and send an e-mail to you with the details of the deal we discussed by noon today."*

You can also signal the end of a call by thanking the person and summarizing the call. For example: *"Thank you for brining this to my attention. Let me go over the dates you gave me to make sure I have them all."*

Don't Always Answer

Nowhere is it decreed that you have to sit up at attention and answer every call that comes in. More a matter of habit than choice, people often answer their phones even when they are in the middle of a project that requires intense concentration. Under these circumstances, let voice mail take the call and listen to your messages on a break from your project.

Have a Business-Only Phone

If you are a home-based business owner, you need a dedicated telephone line that is for business only. This allows you to keep a clear boundary between work and home.

Offer the Option of E-mail

If you think the discussion you are about to have by phone would be just as well served by an e-mail exchange, suggest the caller drop you a message instead.

Organize Your E-mail In-Box

If you've ever tried to find something specific in a cluttered cupboard, you know how time-consuming and frustrating it can be. Plowing through old boxes of junk, piles of paper, and bric-a-brac saved from Auntie Mildred's wedding eats up time and tests your patience. A messy e-mail in-box can create a similar level of dysfunctional clutter and drive you crazy. A few minutes spent organizing your online life now will pay off tenfold in time saved later.

There are two aspects to sorting out your in-box. One is cleaning out and categorizing the e-mail you already have, and the second is managing new e-mails as they arrive.

To begin with, do a housecleaning on your mailbox and delete old messages (including spam) hanging around that you no longer need. Most people have enough memory in their computer to store the entire Library of Congress collection, so it's temping to just keep old e-mail and skip this step. Remember: The tidier your e-mail is, the less time you will spend searching for what you need.

Next, establish an e-mail filing system that makes it relatively easy to find past messages. One method is to set up your e-mail folders to mirror the way you organize your work files. For example, if you generally reference your work by account name, then set up your e-mail folders by account name; if you generally reference by date, then set up your folders by date; and so on.

How many times have you given your attention to the same e-mail (looked at it, opened it, re-read it) and then moved to another task without taking any action? Once you have an orderly in-box, keep new arrivals from muddling your newfound neatness by not letting e-mails linger, in hopes that they will read and answer themselves. Alan Lakein, in his famous book *How To Get Control of Your Time and Life*(Signet, 1989), encouraged people to handle every piece of paper only once. Ditto for e-mails. The simple solution is to deal with every message that comes in—quickly—by taking one of the following actions.

- **Reply.** If the message sparks an action that you can do within a reasonable amount of time (five minutes or less) handle it now. If an instant response is not practical, flag it for action later or move the item to an established "pending" folder, so that it doesn't get ignored or lost down the road. If the item will require a chunk of time to handle (fifteen minutes or longer) you can also open your date book and schedule a specific time to get it done. Be careful not to create too large a backlog of future to-do items. A twice-weekly review of these items, with corresponding action, should keep your "pending" file from overflowing.

- **File.** If the appropriate file does not already exist, create whatever files you need so that you can collect e-mails from the same source, subject, client, or project together.

- **Delete.** In the same way that throwing out an old pile of magazines that has been hanging around your house for six months can be so satisfying, so is deciding *not* to take action on a non-essential e-mail. If the thought of dumping something you might need in the future makes you shudder in fear, here are a few questions you can ask yourself to determine if the item is a keeper or not:

  > Does the message contain important information I can use now or in the future?

  > Does the message relate to an important project, goal, or task I am currently working on?

  > Does the message contain information that's necessary for me to keep for legal or policy reasons?

- **Forward.** If the item in the e-mail is one that can or should be delegated to someone else, send it on its way ASAP. If you need to take action, but also want to include someone else in the message, forward it to him or her now, not later.

Finally, don't use the default "ignore" as a way to deal with incoming messages.Anything you just let sit for too long can become lost in the crowd, a drain on your mental energy, and more mailbox clutter.

Streamline Your E-mail

Knowing how to write e-mails that produce the results you want *and* save time for yourself and others enhances your online productivity. To streamline your e-mails, use the following practices:

Prune Your Prose

According to a recent survey by ClickZ, 60 percent of people at work often read less than half of each e-mail message they receive. To keep your e-mails from ending up in the "dumped due to lack of interest" pile, trim the fat by removing the extraneous fluff and getting right to the heart of the matter. For example, consider the following message, prior to pruning:

> *I was very surprised and encouraged by the meeting we had two days ago regarding the new systems that we plan to introduce in the spring of next year. I feel that everyone who attended the meeting was well prepared, organized, and understood the specific issues of the integration process. As we discussed at the meeting, it is only with all of us collaborating together that we will be able to foresee possible problems and deal with them efficiently as they arise. I look forward to our next meeting which is on Friday the 27th at 9:30am.*

Here is the same message after pruning:

> *Thank you for being so prepared for the systems meeting two days ago. I look forward to working together toward an efficient implementation. Our next meeting is on Friday the 27th at 9:30 a.m.*

Prioritize Your Paragraphs

Although the general rule—shorter is better—applies to most e-mails, some messages are, by nature, meatier than others and take up more space. In that case, the key is to identify your most important piece of information and place it in the first paragraph of your message. This insures that your "A" priority information gets read, even if the rest of the e-mail doesn't. For example, in the following message, paragraph four contains the main point, but is the last piece of information offered.

Dear Ms. Goodlight:

Thank you for your order. The answers to your questions are as follows:

We have over 200 different lamp designs in stock and can order non-stocked items to arrive within one week. All of our lamps are made of the highest quality materials and are guaranteed for two years. Custom designs are available, upon request.

For wholesale customers, we do offer 30 days net payment policy. You can apply for this by contacting Mr. Barney Smith at bsmith@loveourlamps.com. He will send you the proper paperwork to fill out. It usually takes up to two weeks to process an application.

The lamp you have ordered is available in chrome or nickel. Once we know which finish you require, we will ship it to you immediately.

If you have any other questions, please do not hesitate to contact me.

Time Management In An Instant

To make this e-mail more productive and efficient, the paragraphs should be re-ordered as follows so that the information is offered in order of descending importance:

Dear Ms. Goodlight:

Thank you for your order. The lamp you have ordered is available in chrome or nickel. Once we know which finish you require we will ship it to you immediately.

The answers to your questions are as follows:

For wholesale customers, we do offer a 30-days-net payment policy. You can apply for this by contacting Mr. Barney Smith at bsmith@loveourlamps.com. He will send you the proper paperwork to fill out. It usually takes up to two weeks to process an application.

We have over 200 different lamp designs in stock and can order non-stocked items to arrive within one week. All of our lamps are made of the highest quality materials and are guaranteed for two-years. Custom designs are available, upon request.

If you have any other questions, please do not hesitate to contact me.

58

Move Your Body

If you are one of the millions who work at a desk, talk on the phone, or type at a keyboard, you know the pain of a cramped wrist, crimped neck, and tight shoulders. Sitting in the same position hour after hour can be bad for your health—and is a drain on your energy and concentration. Try these simple exercises to give your body a break and your focus a boost. Of course, none of these are a substitute for medical care, and all stretches should be done slowly and gently, and cause no pain! If you have any doubt about whether you can (or should) do these, check with your doctor before moving a muscle.

Upper Back and Shoulders

Place your hands on your shoulders. With your elbows down, push your shoulders back. Hold for 20 seconds. Repeat four times.

Lower Back

Stand up and exhale while you slowly drop your head towards your knees. Allow your hands to drop to your ankles. Hold for five seconds. Inhale while you slowly unwind and return upright. Repeat four times.

Neck

Gently turn your head to the left, looking over your left shoulder, and hold for 10 seconds. Next gently turn your head to the right, looking over your right shoulder, and hold for 10 seconds. Repeat four times.

Wrists

Place your palms together at chest height. Push your palms together while slightly lifting your elbows. Hold for five seconds. While still holding your palms together, rotate your hands down so your fingertips point to the floor. Hold for five seconds and release. Repeat four times.

Back and Hips

Place your palms on your lower back and gently push your chest forward and stretch your upper torso back. Hold for five seconds. Repeat four times.

Legs

Sit in your chair and, holding your abs in, extend your left leg until it is level with your hip. Hold for two seconds. Next, holding your abs in, extend your right leg until it is level with your hip. Hold for two seconds. Repeat two times.

Boost Your Productivity With Exercise

In a study of 200 office workers by the Leeds Metropolitan University in the UK, six out of 10 people surveyed reported that their time-management skills, mental performance, and ability to meet deadlines improved on days when they exercised. The amount of the overall performance boost was about 15 percent, according to Jim McKenna, a professor of physical activity and health at the university.

Get a Good Night's Sleep

If you're having a bad day at work the problem might not be your overbearing boss or cranky co-worker, but a lack of sleep. Consider these:

- A 2007 study released by the University of Florida revealed that a lack of sleep contributes to employees being more tired at work, and also makes them less satisfied.

- One poll, by the National Sleep Foundation, concluded that 80 percent of American adults believe that not getting enough sleep has led to poor performance at work, including problems concentrating, completing a task, and making decisions.

- The same poll showed that 40 percent of Americans are sleeping fewer than seven hours a night during the workweek, and 75 percent of those surveyed reported problems sleeping a few nights a week, often resulting in missed workdays and errors on the job.
- According to the Better Sleep Council, more than 65 percent of Americans lose sleep because of stress.

To improve your snooze and awaken to a better work life try the following:

Sleep on Schedule

Establish a pattern of sleep by going to bed and getting up at roughly the same time each day. This helps your body set an automatic clock that tells it when to go to bed!

Block the Light

The darker your room is, the better you'll sleep. Wear an eye mask, turn off the night-light, and close the door to prevent light from creeping in.

Hot Hint: If you are in a hotel room with a bright digital clock, cover it up with a towel. Even something as simple as the reflected blue light from an alarm clock can hinder your sleep.

Avoid Stimulation

Watching television, working, or even exercising within an hour of going to bed can cause delays in getting to sleep due to overstimulation. Instead, plan a few pre-bedtime rituals (such as soaking in a warm tub, listening to white noise or a relaxation CD, or some light reading) to help prepare your mind and body for rest.

Watch What You Eat and Drink

Drinking caffeinated coffee, tea, or soft drinks late in the day can interfere with your slumber. In addition, eating sugary foods or drinking alcohol might put you to sleep fast, but will often wake you up in the middle of the night. Skip the sugar and try foods that are high in the amino acid tryptophan, such as turkey, low-fat dairy products, bananas, and hummus.

Wear a Pair of Socks

One way the body readies itself for sleep is to widen the blood vessels in the hands and feet to help radiate heat. Research shows that people with cold feet often have trouble falling asleep so, instead of counting sheep, put on a pair of socks.

60

Save Time in Your Personal Life

It's 7:30 in the morning. The twins can't find their shoes for school, this month's mortgage is due *today*, and you need to pack for your plane trip to the annual business bonanza-marketing meeting. Take heart. Even the most harried of working moms and dads can find ways to save time (and sanity) at home. To shave off an average of one to two hours a week, put in place these tried-and-true helpful hints:

- Cook larger-than-needed meals and freeze the leftovers. Defrost them later in the week for quick and easy lunches and dinners.
- Buy Green Bags (*www.greenbags.com*) to store your vegetables and fruit. They keep your produce fresh for up to 30 days and eliminate extra trips to the grocery store.

- Put all the kids' snack stuff (bowls, plates, cups, and so forth) in an easy-to-reach spot so they can help themselves.

- Keep a list and pen by the phone for messages, and another on the fridge for grocery lists. This way you won't have to spend the time searching for one when the need arises.

- Install an instant hot water faucet. Your tea or coffee will be ready in seconds, without having to wait for a kettle to boil.

- Lay out the kids' clothes at night so they're ready in the morning. Do the same for yourself if you will be tight on time in the a.m.

- Use a duvet cover instead of blankets. You can make the bed faster and easier if you eliminate all the straightening and tucking blankets require.

- If you travel frequently, keep a pre-packed bathroom bag ready to go. Keep sample sizes of liquids and gels in a separate plastic bag for airport security.

- Keep a master packing list. You will avoid being scattered and rushed the morning of and avoid arriving at your destination without your hairdryer, electric shaver, or underwear.

- A few days before a trip, figure out all the clothes you will be taking. Try on different mix-and-match combinations so that you can pack as lightly as possible *and* optimize your wardrobe.

- Pay your bills online. Schedule recurring payments (such as mortgage, insurance, credit cards, and so on) so they get paid on the same day every month without you having to lick a stamp, write a check, or go to the post office.

Hot Hint: You can also set up automatic payments, where the company debits the payment automatically from your bank account.

Time Management In An Instant

- Keep a basic cadre of office supplies on hand. Items such as stamps, note cards, return address labels, rubber bands, files, file folders, pens, pencils, paper clips, scissors, and scotch tape are basic to being organized. If this sounds silly, think about the last time you spent time searching for one of these items.

- Set up computer templates for envelopes, letters, and invoices so that you can quickly fill in the blanks and avoid re-creating the same forms over and over.

- Develop checklists for kids to use as a reminder to get things done. For example, a morning chart might include the following: get up, wash face, brush teeth, comb hair, dress, eat breakfast, get school lunch money, get backpack, kiss family good-bye, and catch the bus.

- Get the kids involved in the housework by making it part of their family job. Having the kids help you pick up their toys before lunch/supper will not only get your house clean faster, but teach your children good time-management habits.

- Arrange errands and chores so that they can be done simultaneously. Do the laundry while fixing dinner, or pick up the dry cleaning and do the grocery shopping while a child takes a music lesson.

- Keep a central family calendar clearly visible at home. This allows everyone to see what is coming up the next day, week, and so forth.

Conclusion

When all is said and done, the art of time management is really the art of decision-making. It's the courage to choose what actions you are going to take, when you are going to take them, and how you will get them done. It's about choosing your most important life goals and prioritizing accordingly.

In the day-to-day world of business, these choices happen as part of managing your workflow. Entire books, systems, and programs have been created on the topic, though in essence the idea is elegantly simple:

- Things enter your world from your voice mail, e-mail, snail mail, other people, and your own brain.

- You capture those things in a variety of places, including your to-do lists, in-basket, e-mail, files, and so forth.

- You decide what you are going to do about each of those inputs. Are you going to do them now, do them later, delegate them, or dump them?

- You take the actions necessary to move items through the process until they are done, finished, complete.

Sounds simple, doesn't it? In a way it is, but the discipline and skill necessary to do this require the tools, techniques, and tips offered in this book and others like it. You can become a master at working your workflow. All it takes is practice and commitment—and time!

Index

Index

About the Authors

Keith Bailey and Karen Leland are co-founders of Sterling Consulting Group, an international management consulting firm specializing in maximizing results through the people side of business. In business for 25 years, they have worked with more than 150,000 executives, managers and front–line staff from a wide variety of industries including retail, transportation, hospitality, high-tech, banking and consumer goods.

Their consulting work in corporations and public speaking engagements has taken them throughout North America, Southeast Asia, Africa, and Europe. Their clients have included such companies as AT&T, American Express, Apple Computer, Avis Rent A Car, Bank of America, Bristol-Myers Squibb, The British Government, DuPont, SC Johnson Wax, Lufthansa German Airlines, Microsoft, and Oracle, to name a few.

In addition to their consulting work, Karen and Keith are sought after experts by the media. They have been interviewed by dozens of newspapers, magazines, television and radio stations including: *The Associated Press International, Time, Fortune, Newsweek, The New York Times, Entrepreneur Magazine, Ladies Home Journal, Self* magazine, *Fitness* magazine, CNN, The Today Show, and Oprah.

They are sought-after speakers and have presented for groups such as The Young Presidents Organization, The Society of Association Executives, The Society of Consumer Affairs, and The Direct Marketing Association.

Karen and Keith are the authors of five books, including three editions of the bestselling *Customer Service For Dummies* (Wiley Publishing), which has sold over 200,000 copies and been translated into Spanish, German, Korean, Chinese, and Polish among others. In addition, they are the authors of *Watercooler Wisdom: How Smart People Prosper in the Face of Conflict, Pressure and Change* (New Harbinger, 2006)and *Customer Service In An Instant: 60 Ways to Win Customers and Keep Them Coming Back* (Career Press, 2008).

About Sterling Consulting Group

Sterling Consulting Group offers a variety of training programs, consulting, and keynote speeches. To learn more about our on-site training programs, or to book Karen or Keith to speak at your next event, please visit the Website at *www.scgtraining.com*. For any additional questions or to schedule an interview, contact Karen Leland or Keith Bailey at:

Sterling Consulting Group

180 Harbor Drive #208

Sausalito, CA 94965

(415) 331–5200

kleland@scgtraining.com

www.scgtraining.com